Culture Your Life

Kefir and Kombucha for Every Day Nourishment

Louise Kane Buckley NTP, ND

A Concise Manual for Kefir and Kombucha with over 45 Recipes developed for Health, Strength and Nourishment.

Drinks • Food • Cosmetics • Household

Culture Your Life

Kefir and Kombucha for Every Day Nourishment

Copyright © 2014 by Louise Kane Buckley NTP, ND. 504793

ISBN:
Softcover   9781493132430
EBook   9781493132447

All rights reserved. No part of this book may be reproduced or transmitted in any form or by any means, electronic or mechanical, including photocopying, recording, or by any information storage and retrieval system, without permission in writing from the copyright owner.

....

© Loula Natural

All photos and content belong to Louise Kane Buckley.

This book or any portion thereof may not be reproduced or used in any manner whatsoever without the express written permission of the author Louise Kane Buckley. Permission may be accepted if using a brief quotations or in a book review.

This book is for entertainment purposes. The author of this cookbook is not responsible in any manner whatsoever for any adverse effects arising directly or indirectly as a result of the information provided in this book.

www.loulanatural.com

Rev. date: 11/10/2014

To order additional copies of this book, contact:
Xlibris LLC
1-800-455-039
www.xlibris.com.au
Orders@Xlibris.com.au

"People are raised to view bacteria as dangerous enemies and refrigeration as a household necessity…Bacterial growth triggers fear of danger, disease and even death."

"Moving towards a more harmonious way of life and greater resilience requires active participation."

Become a producer and creator rather than a consumer.

"Food is the greatest community builder there is."

Sandor Ellix Katz
The Art of Fermentation
(Katz, 2012)

"Let food be thy medicine and medicine be thy food."
Hippocrates

Acknowledgements

Without turning this into an Academy Awards speech, there are some people I must thank for helping me put together my first book.

Mickeymoo for seeing into the future, Jacqueline and Kate for reading through all my work and being my sounding boards, Rachele for her picture taking and sketches, Ronie who has helped me develop many of the recipes, everyone who has attended my workshop and been a source of amazing inspiration, my Dad who has taken everything I say on board and supported me, my Mum who would have gotten a real kick out of me writing books and my brother Neil and his lovely Courtney, to whom I hope to give the grains and a SCOBY.

To my editor Diana, thank you for helping get my voice out there!

Of course I want to thank my kids for being my Monkeys, and for my Niall who tastes everything I give him and to whom this is dedicated.

Table of Contents

Acknowledgements vii
Disclaimer xiii

Introduction

Who am I? 2
What is Naturopathy? 4

Fermentation Basics

What is Culturing and Fermentation? 7
Difference Between a Probiotic and Alive Fermented Products. 9
Introduction to the Digestive and Immune Systems 10
Bacteria and Energy production 12
Ingredients used 13
Equipment 17
Alcohol Content of Fermented Foods 19
Storage and Shelf life 20

Chapter 1
KEFIR

What is Kefir? 24
Reported Health Benefits of Kefir 25
5 Reasons to make Kefir 26
Nutritional Constitutes of Milk Kefir: 27
Comparing Bacteria Found in Homemade Kefir to a Commercially Made Kefir. 28
How to Make Kefir: 30
Directions: 31
The Russian Method 32

Chapter 2
KEFIR RECIPES

DRINKS

Lychee Coconut Water Kefir 38
Apple Water Kefir 39
Mango Coconut Water Kefir 40

Clementine & Cinnamon Water Kefir 41
Mixed Berry Water Kefir 42
Cacao & Vanilla Water Kefir 43
Lemon, Honey, Turmeric & Ginger Water Kefir 44
Sunshine Shot 45
Beetroot, Carrot & Apple Water Kefir 47
Pumpkin Pie Water Kefir 48
Blueberry and Vanilla 49
Cucumber and Mint 50
Apple & Fig Water Kefir 51
Pomello Water Kefir 52
Kefir Milkshake (Chocolate, Strawberry and Banana flavours) 53
Banana Bread Kefir 54
Morning Smoothie 56
Dreamy Almond 57
Chocolate Avocado Pudding Kefirshake 59
Watermelon Cooler 60
Carrot with Apple Water Kefir 61
Green Kefir Smoothie 62
Liver Green Kefir Smoothie 63
Coconut Water Kefir Rehydration Drink 64

FOOD

Garlic Kefir Dip 69
Kefir Cheese 72
Lemon Kefir Cheese Cake 73
Kefir Meat Jerky 74
Kefir Soda Bread 75
Banana & Kefir Muffins 77
Nate's Blueberry & Kefir Mauffins 78
Kefir Pancakes 80
Coconut Yoghurt 83
Strawberry Kefir Ice Cream 84
Rocky Road Kefir Ice Cream 86
Mint Chocolate Chip Kefir Ice Cream 87
Kefir Gummies 88

COSMETICS

Why is Kefir so great for cosmetics? 92
Hand Sanitiser 93
Skin Soother 94
Sunburn Soother 95
After Swim Skin Balancerr 96
Kefir Face Mask 97
Kefir Grain Bath Salts/Body Scrub 98
Coconut Water Kefir Hair Rinse 99
Rosemary Tea, Water Kefir & Raw Honey hair rinse 100
Chamomile Tea, Raw Honey and Apple Water Kefir Rinse 101

Chapter 3
KOMBUCHA

What is Kombucha 104
Health Benefits of Kombucha 106
5 Reasons to Brew Kombucha 108
Considerations When Making Kombucha 109
Teas to use 110
What you will need: 111
How to make it 111
Directions 112
Troubleshooting: 112
Second Fermentation 113

Chapter 4
KOMBUCHA RECIPES

DRINKS

Chai Roobios and Orange Black Tea Kombucha 118
Ginger Beer Kombucha 119
Mango Kombucha 120
Ice Lemon Kombucha Tea 121
Mixed Berry White Tea Kombucha 123
Apple and Fig White Tea Kombucha 124
Jasmine and Apple Green Tea Kombucha 125

SCOBY

SCOBY Shake 129
Kombucha Salad Dressing 132

HOUSE

Why is Kombucha such a good cleaning product? 136
Fruit Wash 137
All Purpose Cleaner 138
Washing detergent 139
Spot Remover 140
Bath, Sink & Toilet Cleaner 141

SUPPORT RECIPES

Raw Almond Milk 144
Raw Oat Milk 145
Raw Coconut Milk 146
Chia Porridge 147
Raw Jam 148
Chocolate Avocado Pudding 149
Homemade Chocolate 150
Whole Lemon-ade 151
Apple Sauce 152

RESOURCES

References 154
Works Cited 154
Books 156
Websites with Information and Recipes; 157
Web Stores to get Cultures 158
Further Reading 159

Disclaimer

As a Naturopath, I make recommendations on a one to one and case by case basis. If you are in any way worried about using these products and recipes, it is best to speak to someone who knows your individual needs first. I make the following disclaimer:

The information provided in this book is designed to provide helpful information on the subjects discussed. This book is not meant to be used, nor should it be used, to diagnose or treat any medical condition. For diagnosis or treatment of any medical problem, consult your physician. The publisher and author are not responsible for any specific health or allergy needs that may require medical supervision and are not liable for any damages or negative consequences to any person reading or following the information in this book or resulting from any treatment, action, application or preparation outlined in this book. References are provided for informational purposes only and do not constitute endorsement of any websites or other sources. Readers should be aware that the websites listed in this book may have changed.

Trust your senses, consume only what you feel comfortable consuming and make your choices your responsibility.

INTRODUCTION

Digestive weakness is a very common condition and is present in most cases that I see both professionally and personally. I myself also experienced IBS, blood sugar imbalances and skin irritations for almost ten years. The digestive system is the heart and centre of all health and the ability to digest and assimilate nutrients from our foods undoubtedly makes a huge difference in our bodies and therefore our lives. Fermentation has been a big part of my healing journey and in this book I aim to show you how it could be for you too.

Fermentation is fundamental to bacterial balance and bacterial balance in turn is fundamental to health. This is true for all ages and animal species. Bacteria play an important role in energy production, hormone balance, nutrient absorption from our foods, the ability to then use nutrients in our body, blood sugar balance, weight management, immune function and moderation, liver support, mood, memory and so on. Almost every cell action has bacteria to help it. With our increase in antibiotic usage, sterilisation of our environment, pasteurisation and industrialisation of our food sources, and the decrease in consumption of vital fresh real foods, our bodies and environment are suffering. Fortunately, fermenting can help to make key changes in the body to start to return it to health. By nourishing our body we can make huge structural, physical and emotional changes, so imperative to ultimate wellness.

This recipe book is an integral part of my series on Natural Health and I was inspired to write it by the students in my classes who asked me to compile all the information and recipes that I am constantly creating. With my passion for the subject and excitement at seeing the transformation in clients, family and my own health, a recipe book and manual seemed perfect. After all, building a community is all about sharing. Using Kefir and Kombucha may help you to make big differences in your lifestyle and health too.

Although some of you may find it easy to be creative in the kitchen, others may need a nudge in the right direction. I make most of these recipes regularly and include them in my family's day to day life. All of them are easy to make and use common ingredients that you may already have in your homes. Kefir and Kombucha are a great way to start fermenting and I have included directions for making them and suggestions and recipes to help you start consuming them.

These recipes have been designed to be **Grain and Gluten free**. In some cases I have used nuts, but have shown how to make the recipes **Nut free** by replacing nuts with seed milk or buckwheat/coconut flour or coconut milk. These recipes can also be made **Dairy- free** by substituting the cow or goat's milk Kefir with almond, oat, coconut or other alternative milk Kefir. All the recipes are **Free from Refined Sugar**.

I really hope you enjoy the book and the recipes and I welcome you to the Fermenting Community.

Culture Your Life
Kefir and Kombucha For Every Day Nourishment

Who am I?

By truly using food as medicine I have seen massive changes in my own body in a short space of time, so I am very excited to share, learn and grow with you today.

I have been writing and teaching courses on Nutrition for all ages and goals for years. I have huge passion for educating people to take responsibility for their choices and ability to heal themselves. Fermentation classes are by far among my favourite ones to teach. I also run my own company Loula Natural which is a Naturopathic Practice, I write my blog and for online magazines, and have a series of books to run alongside the subjects I teach. At the same time I am raising my two young kids and running a household! As you can imagine, it's a case of constantly juggling my time and since I am only human I am also constantly aware of my own health. As a result, I love easy ways to stay on top of things.

I have been a Personal Trainer for almost a decade and during that time I have made it a point to include nutrition in my clients' programmes. Writing and teaching courses about nutrition has enabled me to help people understand how they can accelerate their journey towards their goals. In the process I became fascinated with the role food and nutrients play in the body's healing process. I saw first hand how they can be used to treat ailments, prevent illness and benefit the body on all levels. I decided to study for a further three years to gain two diplomas and I became a Naturopath and Nutritional Therapist. During this time I also studied and practised Ear Acupuncture and Bach Flower Remedies.

The most common thing I see across all population groups, especially in children and young adults, are issues stemming from digestive weakness and dysfunction. All the food, nutrients and supplements taken are somewhat useless without the ability to break them down, absorb them and of course use them. Treating and healing the digestive system can in fact right most wrongs experienced in a person's body. From my own chronic issues to my children's seemingly healthy bodies, I guess you could say I'm a little obsessed with healing and supporting a strong, healthy and functional digestive system.

Ever since I left home to go to university I have had an up and down relationship with my digestion and body shape. I put on a lot of weight, mainly on my stomach, and became a classic apple shape. I also changed my diet and had to quickly learn how to cook for myself. I played with trying to be wheat-free (I didn't know about gluten back then) and dairy-free (although at that time soy milk was the only easily available alternative). Throughout the years, even when teaching 10 spin classes a week, I could not shake off my excess weight with the additional challenges of poor blood sugar control and IBS symptoms. I continued to gain and lose weight with a disproportionate amount of weight going on my stomach. Since introducing fermented foods, however (as well as making other lifestyle changes, including recognising and eliminating food intolerances to help reduce inflammation in my body) my body shape has changed and - best of all - my IBS symptoms have dissipated.

In recent years I have made many changes to my own and my family's lifestyles. One of my greatest joys now is to create meals from scratch, filling the food with as many nutrients and as much love as possible. But perhaps my greatest satisfaction comes from knowing that the work I am doing is protecting and supporting the health and well-being of the people who mean so much to me - my family, friends, readers and clients. Fermenting is central to this and I make Kefir and Kombucha in my house regularly.

What is Naturopathy?

"Health is a state of complete physical, mental, and social well-being; not just the absence of disease or infirmity"
— Author Unknown

Naturopathic medicine dates back to classical times when physicians were as interested in food to provide health as they were in understanding the process of disease. It was a time when people nurtured their body, mind and soul and used the plants and elements that surrounded them. There are six principles of Naturopathic Medicine that can help to explain how a naturopath will approach healing. A different approach to healing and one using only natural methods can have huge effect on the body. Methods and rituals that have been used successfully for thousands of years:

Culture Your Life
Kefir and Kombucha For Every Day Nourishment

First Do Not Harm

A Naturopath uses the following guidelines: Use the least force necessary to diagnose and treat. Minimize the risk of harmful side effects. Avoid the suppression of symptoms. Acknowledge, respect and work with the individual's self-healing process. Refer for treatment when your skills are inappropriate. Know your skills and limitations. Work together with other practitioners for the client's safety, with success in mind.

The Healing Power of Nature

The Vital Force is an inherent self-healing process within each of us and we each have our own relationship with it. A Naturopath will give the body space to allow the energy to help remove the obstacles to healing and recovery by identifying the body's signals and delivering options for the individual to come into line with his or her own healing intuition.

Identify and Treat the Cause

A Naturopath will seek to identify the underlying cause or the driver of the illness rather than merely suppressing the symptoms.

Doctor as Teacher

Prevention is better than cure. A Naturopath will educate and encourage patients towards self-responsibility for health by teaching them about their bodies and empowering them to heal themselves.

The Naturopath *supports* the healing; however it's the patient who *does* the healing!

Treat the Whole Person

A Naturopath takes into account all aspects of the individual's life, such as physical, emotional, spiritual, genetic, environmental and social factors, in order to get the whole picture.

Prevention Rather than Cure

A Naturopath emphasises the prevention of disease by assessing the patient's risk factors in terms of heredity and susceptibility to disease and makes appropriate interventions to prevent illness. A commitment is made to create a healthy world where humanity will thrive.

Fermentation Basics

What is Culturing and Fermentation?

Culture comes from the word *cultivate*. Many cultured foods have come from ancient rituals passed down since the dawn of time by peoples of many different cultures and backgrounds. When you cultivate you promote or improve something through work and attention. The base ingredients are enhanced and made more nutritious through fermentation. When we use *culture* as a verb, it means to grow and to introduce. When we grow and introduce our bacterial and yeast starters (whether Kefir grains or a Kombucha SCOBY) to our milks, waters and teas we allow a natural process to occur through which there is a transfer and addition of nutrients (probiotics are beneficial bacteria). Culturing also provides additional means of enhancing the body's ability to absorb and assimilate nutrients.

Fermentation is a change or transformation. For thousands of years, scientists have found documented evidence of cultures consuming foods preserved and altered using micro-organisms, bacteria and yeasts. Most cultures have some kind of fermented food in their food history and many still include a fermented food/drink within their daily meals. When applied to our foods the bacteria and yeasts use the sugars in our foods to grow and create energy. This is how our foods come 'alive'. Our world has become largely dependent on refrigeration and we have largely relegated much of our food production to factories. Mass produced food has meant many changes to the natural growing and distribution of food products. This in turn has affected the make-up, quality and accessibility of nutrients in our foods. It has also contributed to a large proportion of our diet being 'dead'. Take UHT milk, for example. All enzymes and bacteria naturally present in the milk have been killed off, making the milk largely indigestible and essentially a 'dead' product.

Each variation and even each batch of Kefir, Kombucha and yoghurt is slightly different. At a basic level all come from the same starting point (bacteria and yeast), which help to transform, harness and access the vitality and nutrients in our foods. This makes it very difficult for the manufacturing process to accurately reproduce what can be achieved quite easily in a humble kitchen. The ferments that you make in your own kitchen will be influenced by the micro-organisms inside you and in your environment so they will be different from the ferments I make in my kitchen. This makes the case for fermenting for yourself - creating rather than being the consumer. You will receive the micro-organisms from your ferments that you need to maintain balance between yourself and your environment and this is one of the keys to whole body health. It also makes perfect sense to then also use these products in our outer environment (cosmetics, cleaning products and room sprays for easing situations like damp, pollution and irritated skin).

Believe it or not, we are made up of bacteria and micro-organisms. Everything around us is too, and yet we seem to be determined to destroy them. From using hand sanitisers and bleaching the toilet to taking antibiotics for every cold, skin and gastrointestinal complaint, eradicating bacteria seems to be most people's focus. The combination is playing a role in the rise of chronic illnesses in all ages, especially our children. Our human cells are outnumbered by bacteria by something like 9:1 and some reports suggest that bacteria constitute 20 times more mass than cells. There are up to 700 necessary species of bacteria in a 'healthy' oral cavity alone. Also, having intestinal flora is the only way our bodies can make some of the B vitamins and vitamin K, which are so important to our health. Bacteria will never be killed off by humans, and by continuing to believe we need to kill them off we will maintain the bacterial mutations we are now experiencing and more and more chronic conditions and degradation will occur.

Fermented foods are vibrant and we could not exist without our bacterial partners. For example, using whey to soak grains can help our body to digest them. Our digestive system needs them and a healthy digestive system is the root of all health since it is vital for the procurement, absorption and assimilation of nutrients used to power every other body system. Our immune system also depends on these nutrients and we could not use or store energy without them. Bacteria's role in the inflammatory process can help us to address most chronic illnesses (auto-immune conditions, for example, can be the inability to switch off the inflammatory process).

So you can see how important these bacterial partners are in maintaining our health! Of course Kefir and Kombucha are not the only ways to ferment and culture your foods in order to promote the good bacteria. They are just two simple examples of several ways to add fermented products to your life. *Having a portion of any type of fermented food on a daily basis is going to have a profound effect on your body's health.*

Fermentation products come in several different varieties, for example:

Lacto-Fermented (using whey as a starter)
Fermented dairy: cheese, yoghurt, buttermilk, crème fraiche, sour cream
Kefir (milk and water)
Kombucha (fermented tea)
Fermented Soy: Natto, Miso, Tempeh
Cultured vegetables: pickles, capers, Sauerkraut, Kimchi (any fruits and vegetables)
Vinegar fermentation: apple cider, red wine, coconut vinegars
Alcohol fermentation: beer, wine, cider, gin, vodka and whiskey
Meat/fish fermentation: beef jerky, corned beef, smoked salmon, preserved meats, pickled herring and ceviche.
Condiments: ketchup, salsa, relishes, fish sauce, soy sauce and mustard.
Kvass made from beetroot
Grains: dahl, dosa, rejuvelac, sprouting
Oils: fermented cod liver oil, skate oil and sesame oil

Fermenting is a natural phenomenon. Very little is actually understood about the make-up of the starters (kefir grains or SCOBY's) and how they grow, transform and multiply (t.-H. Chen, 2009). Some do it spontaneously and some are seemingly indestructible. The transformative power of fermentation can produce alcohol, which can help to preserve our foods and make them more digestible, less toxic and more delicious.

A frequently asked question is: *"How will I know which are the 'good' bacteria?"*

My answer is: They are all good and they are all necessary. It is the ratio, amount and the environment they are in that makes the difference. It all depends on the soil (food) and the internal and external environment that determines growth and development of all species.

DIFFERENCE BETWEEN A PROBIOTIC AND ALIVE FERMENTED PRODUCTS.

As I have said before, fermentation as a system for preserving has been around for thousands of years. It is said that soldiers in Ghengis Khan's army received fermented foods as rations, Cleopatra supposedly bathed in fermented milk, and some say that yoghurt actually first came from sheep herders carrying milk in their cloth bags around their waist. It's really important to appreciate that probiotics for health is not a new concept. However it is a new concept to buy and take them in pill form. Recent media coverage suggests that fermentation is the new way to boost the immune system but actually it is the most ancient method documented throughout history!

"Let food be thy medicine and medicine be thy food" Hippocrates

Fermented foods are also alive (and not freeze dried as in the capsules) so are ready to inhabit and balance the bacteria in your digestive system. A fermented product will contain the probiotic strains together with other key nutrients such as lactic acid, which plays a fundamental role in their utilisation by the body. Capsules may help promote good bacteria but will not take up residence like Kefir does. Also, Kefir has on average 35 strains of alive bacteria working together in symbiosis. How many strains are listed on the back of your probiotic capsules?

"Fermented foods not only give you a wider variety of beneficial bacteria, they also give you far more of them, so it's a much more cost effective alternative. Here's a case in point: It's unusual to find a probiotic supplement containing more than 10 billion colony-forming units. But when my team actually tested fermented vegetables produced by probiotic starter cultures, they had 10 trillion colony-forming units of bacteria. Literally, one serving of vegetables was equal to an entire bottle of a high potency probiotic! So clearly, you're far better off using fermented foods". Natasha Campbell McBride (Mcbride, 2010)

Live bacteria are safe for everyone, can be taken while pregnant and are great for babies too.

Another interesting topic is also seen here:

"A clinical study conducted with infants who received either a mixture of pre/probiotic or placebo showed weight gain only in infants who received the pre/probiotic mixture". Rosa Krajmalnik-Brown, 2012, Feb 24th

Introduction to the Digestive and Immune Systems

"Comparative studies based on the germfree gut have provided clear evidence that the gut microbiota is instrumental in promoting the development of both the gut and systemic immune systems. Early microbial exposure of the gut is thought to dramatically reduce the incidence of inflammatory, autoimmune and atopic diseases, further fuelling the scientific viewpoint that microbial colonization plays an important role in regulating and fine-tuning the immune system throughout life." (Kelly D, 2007)

To understand the benefits you can expect from using fermented foods in your diet, it is useful to have an understanding of the two body systems and how they are directly impacted by adding beneficial bacteria.

Without a properly functioning Digestive System (of which breaking down foods, taking in nutrients and eliminating waste products are the main roles) optimal health is almost impossible to achieve. It truly is the root of all health and an intricate and fascinating system that is only now being fully understood. Bacteria are at the centre of this. Not only do they help provide us with Vitamin B12, K, and bile salts for fat metabolism, they also help to digest carbohydrates and proteins. Bacteria out-number our cells by almost 10:1 and every strain ('bad' or 'good') has a role within the body. It is the ratio and the environment they are given that determines whether they thrive or go renegade.

Our largest link to the environment around us is through the Digestive System. Essentially a long tube with two openings (mouth and anus) it is closed to the outside world but is intrinsically linked to all other body systems through messages and nutrients from the world around us (hormones and nerve regulators play a vital role in this). The Nervous, Immune and Endocrine systems all rely on these messages and nutrients in order to function optimally. The digestive system is also the body's primary way to eliminate toxins and waste products produced by the body and the environment.

Even if you consume a densely nutritious diet with supplements, a sub-optimal digestive function means you may have impaired nutrient absorption (especially of such vital nutrients as essential fats, amino acids, calcium, iron, magnesium vitamin C, D, A, E and zinc), impaired energy production, hormonal imbalance, a compromised intestinal lining which is also called leaky gut (leading to possible allergies and intolerances as foods escape without proper procedure into the body), dysbiosis (imbalance of bacteria and microbes) and inflammation. Research suggests that the re-introduction of bacteria can help to rebalance and heal some of these symptoms of dis-ease.

The Immune system is hugely complex and is intrinsically linked to the digestive system. Around 85% of your immune system is provided by the digestive system. Bacteria's role in the immune system is not only to help the digestive system to procure nutrients necessary for cell growth and repair but also to signal any imbalance, mounting a defence and also having a direct effect on the production of immune cells. The use of nutrients and bacteria from fermented foods to stimulate and regulate the immune system is being researched as a more effective way of providing health and vitality.

The immune system is viewed as the body's way of mounting a defence against environmentally imbalanced bacteria and other pathogens. However, we are constantly breathing in some 14,000 germs and bacteria per hour. If bacteria make up almost ten times our actual cells, why are we so intent on eradicating them? If germs are so harmful, why aren't we all dead? By reintroducing balanced bacteria, eating whole foods, and reducing chemicals and toxins in our lives, our immune system will not be as overworked. By managing stress and encouraging the body to go into active relaxation mode, we allow the inflammatory process to regulate, thus reducing the damage chronic inflammation can cause.

Below is a summary of two ways of looking at the body and why we get 'sick'. One is based on the work of Bechamp and the other on the work of Pasteur. Bechamp was a contemporary of Pasteur and some even say that Pasteur may have plagiarised and reworded Bechamp's theory. Naturopaths commonly refer to Bechamp's theory, while pharmaceutical medicine is largely based on Pasteur's germ theory. Bechamp's cellular theory promotes the individual's responsibility for the soil within the body as the basis of health and strength, while Pasteur's theory negates the individual's responsibility for health and encourages reliance on pharmaceuticals to do the work.

GERM THEORY (PASTEUR)	CELLULAR THEORY (BECHAMP).
1. Disease arises from micro-organisms outside the body.	Disease arises from micro-organisms within the cells of the body.
2. Micro-organisms are generally considered to be something to be guarded against.	These intracellular micro-organisms normally function to build and assist in the metabolic processes of the body.
3. The function of micro-organisms is constant.	The function of these organisms changes to assist in the catabolic (disintegration) processes of the host organism when that organism dies or is injured. This may be chemical as well as mechanical.
4. The shapes and colours of micro-organisms are constant.	Micro-organisms change their shapes and colours to reflect the medium.
5. Every disease is associated with a particular micro-organism.	Every disease is associated with a particular condition.
6. Micro-organisms are primary causal agents.	Micro-organisms become "pathogenic" as the health of the host organism deteriorates. Hence, the condition of the host organism is the primary causal agent.
7. Disease can "strike" anybody.	Disease is built by unhealthy conditions.
8. To prevent disease we have to "build defences".	To prevent disease we have to create health.

BACTERIA AND ENERGY PRODUCTION

There are several current studies into ways of using bacteria as a natural renewable fuel source. The following gives some insight into how this would also work within the human body.

Most of the digestive system's bacteria are found in the large intestine. This is where most of the micro and macro nutrients have already been absorbed in the small intestine and where most of the water is being pulled back out to make the stool ready to be eliminated. Fermentation that occurs here is complex and very necessary.

The primary function of bacteria and fermentation is to try and release energy from the densely fibrous carbohydrates left over from digestion higher up the system. Acids such as butyrate and others that are essential for the liver (propionate) and muscles (acetate) are also thought to be manufactured here along with short chain fatty acids essential to the body's methods of energy production (citric acid chain or the electron transport system). The B vitamins, vitamin K and some bile acids are also made here. These are all essential to health and energy production.

"The microbes present within the gastrointestinal tract (i.e. gut microbiota) have coevolved with the human host to perform a number of functions the host would otherwise be unable to accomplish on its own...The genes involved in the metabolism of starch, sucrose, glucose, galactose, fructose, arabinose, mannose, and xylose, as well as fucose from host mucus, are enriched in the distal colon microbiome." (Rosa Krajmalnik-Brown, 2012, Feb 24th)

It would therefore make sense that, along with increasing energy consumption, the correct balance of bacteria can also help the body back to its ideal weight, whether that necessitates weight gain or loss. It also will support lean muscle mass growth and repair. This seems to further enforce the idea that healthy weight maintenance is about more than merely 'calories in and calories out'.

Bacteria support the liver by helping to produce essential acids and creating energy, this in turn can help balance hormone levels. Also, by controlling the amount of sugar in the blood stream, bacteria support insulin sensitivity and balance blood sugar. By encouraging a more cultured palate by consuming fermented foods (especially Kombucha) you are also minimising sugar cravings. By encouraging the bile salt production, fermented foods can also help digest fats and the overall increased nutrient absorption supports the body to regulate metabolism and hormone production. This will in turn help support the positive body shape. In particular, creating a bacterial balance can help to reduce the 'apple' shape attributed to hormone (particularly insulin) imbalance. It also helps reduce digestive bloating and can help you to achieve that flat stomach or reduce a muffin top.

Ingredients used

It is important to mention that common sense and basic hygiene should be observed when preparing your containers, utensils and foods for fermentation. Foods should be clean and pesticide free if possible. Use Kombucha vegetable wash (recipe in book) or apple cider vinegar to wash out your containers and equipment before using. Sanitising containers/utensils before adding bacteria seems to be counterintuitive. However, if you have recently used something to ferment raw animal products it makes sense to ensure that it is clean before using it for a vegetable ferment. This should be taken as basic hygiene, in the same way you wash your hands before preparing food.

When choosing your ingredients for any of the recipes in this book, try and use the highest quality that you have access to. I try to use ingredients that are:

Organic: Not only are organic foods reputed to have higher nutrient values (being potentially more likely to be grown in soil with a higher mineral content from natural fertilisers) and superior taste. USDA organic stipulates that:

Organic foods (be) produced by farmers who emphasize the use of renewable resources and the conservation of soil and water to enhance environmental quality for future generations. Organic meat, poultry, eggs, and dairy products come from animals that are given no antibiotics or growth hormones. Organic food is produced without using most conventional pesticides; fertilizers made with synthetic ingredients *or sewage sludge; bioengineering; or ionizing radiation.* (organic.com FAQ)

Grass-Fed: (where appropriate): When an animal is allowed to eat the foods it is naturally inclined to eat, the meat is more likely to be healthy and contain the nutrients it is claimed to have. This is true also of all dairy and dairy products (milk, butter, cheese and cream) from all dairy producing animals (cows, sheep and goats).

Full Fat: Fat is necessary to life and holds many nutrients. By skimming the fat we are removing a key component of a natural product and leaving a gap in its nutrient status.

Free range: Hens allowed to range freely and eat a natural diet will provide eggs containing all the vitamins and minerals that make eggs Nature's perfect package.

Non-GMO: My motto is: "Only natural food for me". Anything that has been manipulated may not be recognised by the body as food and the body may mount an immune attack on it. The reasons for rejecting GMO (Genetically Modified Organisms) are vast and well documented.

Raw: This is important for all nuts, milks (although raw dairy milk is unavailable in some countries), coconut water, coconut meat, fruit and vegetables for smoothies and yoghurts in order to provide as many enzymes and nutrients as possible to aid digestion.

Soaked: This is necessary in the case of nuts and seeds in order to remove the indigestible layer naturally surrounding them that protects the nutrients which are needed to promote growth of a new plant.

Homemade: In the case of dehydrated fruit, chocolate, nut/seed, oat and coconut milks and Kefir and Kombucha, I prefer to make them at home so that I have control over all the ingredients added. Most nuts and seeds make a delicious milk/Kefir. However, I mostly prefer to use: almond, hazelnut, cashew, hemp, pumpkin or sunflower seeds or combinations of these.

Concentrated essences: I prefer to use concentrated essences like the brand Medicine Flower because they use natural substances, are cold pressed and 100% pure. When using these essences, follow the directions on the bottle. Be cautious, however, with essences and try if possible to use the *actual* food such as vanilla pod or spice powders. Many essences contain synthesised chemicals and I advise you to avoid them if possible.

Dairy Milk; cow, goat or sheep, whichever is your preference. When milk was from the 'neighbour's cow', it was liquid gold. The cow was put out to pasture, ate what it was naturally led to eating, produced offspring and provided milk at a reasonable level. It was full of nutrients, bacteria and good fats, proteins, vitamins and minerals. Those who have access to raw milk will understand what I am talking about.

Sadly, this 'neighbour's cow' rarely exists today. For the most part cows are forced into cramped spaces, fed an unnatural diet and milked constantly. They are exposed to (amongst other things) synthetic hormones and antibiotics. Organic milk is different in this respect, but even organic milk is then homogenised. This regulates the size and distribution of the fat molecules, potentially making the milk more digestible but causing an unnaturally high level of fat and protein to be absorbed into your bloodstream. (This can potentially cause irritation and inflammation, especially for those more prone to lactose intolerance). Try and buy grass-fed raw milk if available.

Skimmed milk is also fortified with nutrients that are lost through taking out the fat and leaving a sugar and water solution. Pasteurisation then indiscriminately kills off all the enzymes and bacteria in the milk. The action of the bacteria and enzymes is crucial to the digestive system's ability to help break down and use whatever nutrients may be left in the milk. Raw milk left outside will turn into sour milk. UHT and pasteurized milk without a micro-organism, starting point will spoil as the internal and external environments are unable to balance. This therefore develops an unbalanced bacterial environment which may cause further disruption in the body. This is before you take into account the stress hormones that the cows produce from being cramped, over-milked and malnourished and the fact that they are not allowed to feed their young.

The process of homogenisation has been developed because mass produced milk is a blend of milk from different farms. Because milk has to be as labelled they have to ensure for example that the milk contains 2 percent fat. This means that they have to regulate the mixed milks. The taste also has to be regulated so that each batch tastes exactly the same. Homeogenisation passes the milk through small holes at high pressure to regulate the fat molecules so that the milk no longer separates with a layer of cream (the best bit of fresh milk.) The emulsified fat then works differently in the body as the process de-naturises it and makes it less absorbable. However regulated milk works well to make creamy yoghurt or kefir and the consistency will be the same with each ferment but I prefer the flavour and more natural state of un-homogenised milk.

The demand for milk has far outweighed supply yet supermarket fridges are full of it. How can this be? The answer is that cows are being milked more than they should naturally be, often resulting in mastitis for the animal and pus finding its way into the milk. In addition, a lot of the milk on sale is not of a high quality since it is often blended from the output of different farms. I would also suggest that you check the labels carefully. What is called 'Milk Drink' is reconstituted milk made from powder (a bit like formula).

More disturbingly, most milk sold in supermarkets is UHT (Ultra-high-temperature) treated, a process that again kills many of the enzymes and bacteria necessary for digestion of the milk. By fermenting milk we are closer to harnessing its naturally available nutrients, making what was a dead product come back to life.

This information is true for all animal milk (goat and sheep too). Ensure you research your milk source.

Water: the best available water is from a spring or well that is rich in minerals and has not been tampered with. However, with very little of that water naturally available without buying it in soft plastic bottles, I choose to use filtered water to make my water Kefir. I ensure that my filter removes chlorine and fluoride as both can have an effect on the grains. I also use a filter that replaces essential minerals. Alternatively, you could use distilled water and then re-mineralise it. Beware also of reverse osmosis or alkalising water filters. This is also true in soft water areas. You can easily buy testing strips but Kefir ideally likes to be in a ph of 4.6. Adding some unwaxed organic lemon can improve your ferment.

Here is a hierarchy of ingredients;

Lowest nutrient value		Highest nutrient value
UHT non-organic milk	Fresh, Organic and un-homogenised milk	Raw milk
White granulated sugar, Xylitol, liquid stevia, agave (highly processed sugars)	Brown sugar	Maple syrup, coconut sugar/nectar, molasses, dates, raw honey, stevia plant leaves
Non-local, non organic fruit and vegetables especially the 'dirty dozen'	Non-organic locally produced 'clean fifteen'	Locally produced, organic produce
Ground nuts/seeds in cellophane packaging	Whole nuts, raw, non organic	Organic, raw whole nuts in foil packaging and refrigerated. Then soaked and sprouted
White flour, Potato flour, Flour blends	Organic Wholemeal flour, Brown Rice flour	Buckwheat flour, Quinoa Flour, Coconut flour, almond flour

What you use has to suit your lifestyle, budget and preferences. By fermenting these products you are always taking them a step higher in nutrient value and quality. Please adjust as appropriate.

All of these recipes can be made **Dairy Free** by substituting dairy with coconut, oat or nut/seed alternatives.

All of these can be made **Nut Free** by supplementing any nuts for seeds or coconut.

All recipes are **Grain Free** and **Gluten Free**. However you can use grains as a substitute if you wish

Recipes containing egg can be made with egg substitutes (such as chia or flax or banana) to be **Egg Free**.

Kombucha will still **contain caffeine** from the tea; however this can be reduced by using a second fermentation and using less Kombucha than water in the dilution.

The bacteria and yeasts naturally present in Kombucha and Kefir will consume the sugar in the recipes so they can be considered **low in sugar**.

Equipment

For both Kefir and Kombucha there is nothing really special about the equipment that is required. The acidity levels of your liquid are quite high, however, so aluminium pans or spoons are not advised as corrosion may occur and this could taint the product. Stainless steel is potentially safe, but I share this quote from *The Art of Fermentation* by Sandor Katz.

"In general, it is best to avoid fermenting in metal containers, at least for the acidic ferments. The reason is that the acids…corrode metals, and the corrosion goes into the food. Theoretically, stainless steel resists corrosion…however it is important to understand that unlike the industrial grade solid stainless steel used in specialised products, most household stainless steel has a thin stainless coating and corrosion can occur anywhere it gets scratched."

Katz also mentions that you can store the liquids for short periods of time in stainless steel. Therefore if you feel comfortable using a metal strainer that's your choice. I use and recommend a plastic strainer so that there is no chance of corrosion. Plastic has its own issues too of course, so I prefer to store my liquids and grains in glass.

Ceramic, glass and cloth are the traditional materials used. However, if metal works for you then it will be better than not fermenting at all!

The fermentation process naturally produces carbon dioxide and so the build up of gas while fermenting in a closed vessel should be taken into account. The potential of the gas to explode out of the top when opened or whilst fermenting is very real and because of this I prefer to ferment in open vessels, which I have purchased. There are many pressure-tested purpose-made products that can be bought if you want to experiment. However, I find that fermenting my Kombucha and Kefir in open vessels creates enough fizz, while further, slower fermentation (which occurs with refrigeratation) gives a good fizz to my Kefir, which I prefer to consume neat. I do not need my brewed Kombucha to contain a lot of natural fizz because I brew it very tart and concentrated and dilute it with fizzy water. I use glass jars with a spigot for dispensing my Kombucha and Kefir brews and I use muslin cloths to cover the jars while fermenting.

Here is a basic list of necessary equipment:

- Glass jars of various sizes (normally 1 litre for Kefir and 1.5/2 litres for Kombucha)
- Measuring jugs and spoons (to measure sugar, liquid volume etc.)
- Plastic strainer or wooden slatted spoon to strain the grains(Kefir only)
- Various bowls to use when straining (Kefir only)
- Wooden chopsticks (stirring Kefir only)
- Teapot (Kombucha only)
- Plastic/wooden spoons to handle grains/SCOBY

It is really useful to document your ferments in a journal to help you to work out a system that suits you. Make a note of ingredients used, amounts of grains and volume of liquid. Then also take into account the temperature, humidity levels and weather. Record the time it takes and any tasting notes. You will find this helpful when trying to replicate flavours or consistency of your ferments.

Alcohol Content of Fermented Foods

One of the by-products of the conversion of sugar by the bacteria and yeasts is the production of alcohol. How much alcohol depends on how much sugar is in the liquid you are fermenting. Generally in these relatively short ferments (especially in the 12 hours needed to make Kefir) there is not enough sugar to produce a large amount of alcohol. Typically you are looking at an alcohol content of under 1%.

In some countries an alcohol content of less than 1% is considered non-alcoholic (e.g. in the EU, Canada and Hong Kong) and a drink with 1% and under will not need to have its % alcohol content stated on the label. However in the US any amount of alcohol present must be shown on the label. It is also the alcohol content that extends the product's shelf life and keeps the drink safe to drink. If you do not want to drink alcohol in any amounts (even naturally occurring) then Kefir (and Kombucha) may not be for you.

There is also a growing trend for making Kefir and Kombucha cocktails, and I have included some recipes which are nice for those occasions when a little tipple is needed. However, please remember that the alcoholic content of the drink will be slightly higher based on the naturally forming alcohols already present. So please moderate additional alcohol and consume responsibly.

The labelling laws:

Australia:
- If over 1.15% alcohol, this should be expressed in mL/100mL or X% alcohol by volume
- If content is between 0.5 and 1.15%, labels should state "contains not more than X% alcohol by volume"

Canada:
- A beverage containing 1.1% or more alcohol by volume is considered an alcoholic beverage. These products must meet the labelling and compositional requirements

EU:
- The labelling of beverages containing more than 1.2% by volume of alcohol must indicate the actual alcoholic strength by volume, i.e. showing the word "alcohol" or the abbreviation "alc." followed by the symbol "% vol."

United States:
- Alcohol content expressed as percent alcohol by volume

If you are concerned about the alcohol content, then I advise diluting the drinks with filtered water, fizzy water or coconut water

Storage and Shelf life

Since fermenting is traditionally the way to preserve foods for when food is scarce in the winter it makes sense that these foods should be stored in a cool environment and have a long shelf life. When your Kefir and Kombucha is to your taste and you have strained your grains and removed your SCOBY, the resulting drinks should be kept in the fridge or a cool dry place to pause fermentation. I have had both in the fridge for extended periods of time without noticing much difference in taste (sometimes up to six months for some Kombucha).

Your body's senses are attuned to whether something is good for you or not. Use your sense of smell and taste to decide whether to consume something and always rely on your own judgement. If you decide not to consume it consider using it for one of the many cosmetic or household recipes or pour it down the sink (thus populating our environment and water supply with beneficial bacteria).

Grains should be stored in the fridge. I store mine dry (without adding sugar and water as many recommend). If you are going to be away for an extended period of time I also recommend freezing a portion of grains and a portion of SCOBY. Alternatively you may also consider dehydrating some grains or SCOBY. These can then be stored in an airtight container. This can ensure that if anything happens to your stock you always have back-up. Simply allow your starters to defrost/rehydrate and return to room temperature. They may need a little TLC for the first couple of ferments after defrosting.

Starters can also be taken with you when you travel. I have taken my kefir grains all over the world with me. I stored them in a small sealed container which I then double bagged them for safety from leaking. I stored them in my check in bags. Please be aware some countries are stricter with their food laws so I generally travel with water grains rather than my dairy milk grains. I can always use my water grains to ferment milk when I get there. Please be advised to declare your grains if you feel it is appropriate. Also actively seek local fermentations; you will get some amazing inspiration this way.

Chapter 1
KEFIR

What is Kefir?

From left to right; Water and Milk Kefir Grains, using milk grains to ferment fresh raw almond milk, straining Milk Kefir

What is Kefir? Simply it is a mix of yeasts and bacteria that live in harmony. Although the starters are called 'grains' they do not contain any grain (for example wheat, rye, spelt, etc.) and are therefore gluten free.

Kefir grains, whether water or milk, are essentially grains of cultured beneficial bacteria. It is what they then go into (a base of either water or milk together with the culture) that determines them as one or the other. After the first fermentation straining process, a little of the starting product is left within the grains.

'Milk Kefir' grains may be used to culture any milk (cow, goat, sheep, soy, rice, any nut/seed or coconut). 'Water Kefir' grains are used to culture water (sugared water, juice or coconut water). With time and patience one type of grain can also be used to culture the other liquid base. The nutrient constituents of the two types of grains will differ based on the liquid they are fermenting. I find the grains are best rotated around liquids. For example, water grains used in coconut water, coconut sugar, maple syrup and dried fruit and stored in the same container yield strong grains with a dense nutrient profile.

The grains may produce different results every time they are used. It is possible that no two batches will be the same, even if the same ingredients are used. It can depend on a number of factors. For example, what has previously cultured (in terms of both the ingredient hierarchy and the base product used, i.e. water or milk) may affect the next batch of Kefir and the grains constituents. The climate (for example, cooler temperatures may result in a longer ferment), humidity (for example, damper environments may mean a shorter time to ferment), the amount of agitation during fermentation (Kefir grains like to be moved and stirred), the size of the grains (size may affect the time needed to ferment) and many other factors may affect the end product.

REPORTED HEALTH BENEFITS OF KEFIR

Stimulation of the immune system

Inhibition of tumour growth

Treatment and prevention of gastrointestinal disorders and vaginal infection. Kefir can work on the unbalanced bacteria that is often present in our foods by helping to balance bacterial environment within the body.

Improved lactose digestion: since the lactose in milk is processed by the bacteria, Kefir becomes a drink that those who are lactose intolerant may be able to digest and is often said to be lactose free.

Improved gluten digestion for those who are not suffering from celiac disease.

May help to reduce cholesterol levels.

May have an influence on the metabolic rate, creating energy and where energy is stored (Backhed, 2004).

May help speed up the recovery period from coughs, colds and flu symptoms as well as gastrointestinal disruptions.

May help to relieve the symptoms of eczema, psoriasis, nappy rash or other skin rashes.

Weight loss and body shape change.

May help to balance hormone levels, especially blood sugar balance and PMS, PCOS symptoms.

Helps the immune system to moderate inflammation especially in the digestive system. This may help repair leaky gut conditions. Also by moderating the immune system, allergies and intolerances have been reported to be decreased.

(This information has been sourced from Farnworth, (2006) and from anectdotal evidence)

5 Reasons to make Kefir

1. Kefir is vibrant and alive. It is vital for the healthy functioning of our digestive system, which in turn affects every other body system, especially our immune system. We would not exist without our bacterial partners and we could not use or store energy without them.

2. Kefir is a natural probiotic. Kefir grains are essentially cultured beneficial bacteria in a base of either milk or water. With time and patience product from either method may be used to culture either or both. The drinks are safe for almost all ages. Kefir can be taken while pregnant and is great for babies (just be sure not to give dairy milk kefir before the age of one).

3. Kefir is cheaper than bottled probiotics. In addition, there could be as many as 35 strains of beneficial bacteria in Kefir, which are alive and in the right ratio with each other. As a comparison, check how many strains are listed on the back of your bottle of probiotic capsules. The live bacteria from Kefir are ready to inhabit and balance the bacteria in your digestive system. Probiotic capsules, on the other hand, may contain only a few selected strains that have been freeze dried. These capsules may help promote good bacteria but will not take up residence in the way that Kefir does.

4. Kefir is very easy to make. You need a liquid containing sugar, a warm environment (room temperature) and Kefir grains. All you do is add the grains to the liquid, leave for between 12-24 hours, strain and then use. Other forms of fermenting can take longer and be a bit more temperamental! The grains are virtually indestructible and can be stored easily in the fridge. The Kefir community is inclusive and open to all so you should be able to find grains from someone in your area. (The grains are meant to be free, but some people may charge postage or a nominal fee.)

5. Kefir can be used in many ways – for example: in smoothies, yoghurt, pancakes, ice cream and green drinks - and it also has many cosmetic benefits. The possibilities are endless! Use Kefir on your skin and see how great it is for eczema. With an additional fermentation (typically named the second fermentation) the possibilities for goodness, nutritional content and taste are even greater.

Nutritional Constitutes of Milk Kefir:

(Farnworth, 2006)
Microorganisms: lactic acid bacteria, yeasts
Fermentation products: carbon dioxide, ethanol (alcohol)
Nutrients: protein from milk, polysaccharide
Vitamins or pro-vitamins: vitamin A, vitamin B1, vitamin B2, vitamin B6, vitamin D, folic acid, nicotinic acid
Minerals: calcium, iron, iodine
Water

What constitutes Kefir and its nutritional density depends greatly on the type of liquid being fermented and the constituents within the liquid.

When milk (or any juice or yoghurt - or canned or bottled product for that matter) is pasteurised the enzymes present in the milk (which are necessary to uptake nutrients, for example calcium) are destroyed and so the milk becomes a "dead" product. By reintroducing bacterial life you re-energise the milk (making it bio-active and its nutrients more bio-available) and therefore make potential nutrients available for absorption.

Coconut water is a great example of a perfect balance of nutrients, enzymes and the bacteria necessary for their absorption. In some ways it can be compared to an egg yolk as it supplies all the nutrients needed to provide growth, strength and nourishment for a coconut tree. The water, combined with the fat from the meat, makes the coconut a great nutritional package. Once the coconut water is pasturised and put in a carton however (even though nothing else is added) the enzymes and bacteria necessary for absorption are killed off, making the liquid no better than a concentrated juice in my opinion. Through fermentation you can unlock the nutrients within the liquid again. Therefore, I see no real benefit in fermenting pure (straight from the coconut) coconut water since in itself it is perfect. However, I do not consume packaged coconut water (or indeed juices) unless it has been fermented.

In this respect Kefir is known as a functional food.

"One that is consumed as part of a usual diet, and is demonstrated to have physiological benefits and/or reduce the risk of chronic disease beyond basic nutritional functions"
(Farnworth, 2006)

For this and other reasons, I use:

Organic un-homogenised milk to make my **Dairy Milk Kefir** (When possible use raw milk)

Pasturised cartons of coconut water for my **Coconut Water Kefir**

Homemade almond milk for my **Almond Milk Kefir**

Coconut sugar/maple syrup/coconut nectar and filtered water to make **Water Kefir**

Comparing Bacteria Found in Homemade Kefir to a Commercially Made Kefir.

The bacteria will feed on the lactose in the milk and the sugar in the water (coconut or juice). The result is always a natural probiotic that is far superior to a bottled one in terms of quality (see comparison below) and is therefore a natural antibiotic.

When using grains that have been passed on from the fermenting community, which are alive, which have been growing in good quality base liquids and have been allowed to multiply by being left to their own devices, it may be very difficult to control the end product. Therefore, each batch may be slightly different, depending on what you are fermenting, the length of time, and the environment you are fermenting in.

When you want to sell a product you have made, there are very strict licensing laws. For example, there needs to be some control over the amount of alcohol the grains are producing. (Some strains of bacteria/yeasts are specifically eliminated.) The environment and starting liquids need to be controlled and monitored so that a consistent product is achieved on a production line and on a commercial scale. Store-bought Kefir is almost never strained. Instead the culture is added rather as it is in yoghurt production. This is another method of controlling and speeding up production.

This in turn may change the probiotic content of the finished product. Also check the amount of sugar the product contains. Homemade Kefir contains very little sugar after the fermentation process but commercial companies sometimes add sugar to their finished Kefir to enhance flavour.

I believe that the advantage of using homemade, strained, alive and natural Kefir is that you have all of the bacteria strains present in their natural states and ratios allowing them to work together in symbiosis. I recommend that when making these recipes you use homemade Kefir fermented by you as the creator. If this is impossible, however, using the store bought products may add probiotic benefit to your life and so can be used if necessary.

From Left to Right; Milk Kefir, Water Kefir and Coconut Water Kefir

Bacterial Contents of Kefir made from Heritage Grains that are then Strained
(Farnworth, 2006)

Lactobacilli
Lactobacillus kefir a,c,j,n,o,p,r Lactobacillus delbrueckii a,h,p
Lactobacillus kefiranofaciens l,n,p Lactobacillus rhamnosus a,r
Lactobacillus kefirgranum n Lactobacillus casei h
Lactobacillus parakefir n,o Lactobacilli paracasei p
Lactobacillus brevis g,h,p,r Lactobacillus fructivorans k
Lactobacillus plantarum o,p Lactobacillus hilgardii k
Lactobacillus helveticus a,b,h Lactobacillus fermentum r
Lactobacillus acidophilus g,p,r Lactobacillus viridescens r
Lactococci
Lactococcus lactis subsp. lactis a,c,e,f,g,h,k,o,r
Lactococcus lactis subsp. cremoris a,e,f
Streptococci
Streptococcus thermophilus e,h
Enterococci
Enterococcus durans d*,e*
(reported as Streptobacterium durans in ref. d; reported as
Streptococcus durans in ref. e)
Leuconostocs
Leuconostoc sp. r
Leuconostoc mesenteroides a,b,g*,o
(reported as Leuconostoc kefir in ref. g)
Acetic acid bacteria
Acetobacter sp. o
Acetobacter pasteurianus g*
(reported as Acetobacter rancens in ref. g)
Acetobacter aceti a,d
Other bacteria
Bacillus sp. r Micrococcus sp. R, Bacillus subtilis g Escherichia coli r

Bacterial Contents found in a Bottled Fermented Probiotic Drink:

Bifidobacterium breve ssp. breve,
bifidobacterium infantis ssp. infantis,
bifidobacterium longum,
enterococcus faecalis TH10, lactobacillus acidophilus, lactobacillus brevis, lactobacillus bulgaricus, Lactobacillus casei spp. casei, lactobacillus fermentum, lactobacillus helveticus ssp. jugurti, lactobacillus plantarum,
streptococcus thermophilus.

How to Make Kefir:

While Water/Milk Kefir grains are seemingly indestructible, they may be sensitive to extreme temperatures so try and bring what you are fermenting, and your grains, to room temperature before combining and **keep away from heat**. Remember, by choosing ingredients on the high up end of the hierarchy you will produce a more nutrient dense product. Using ingredients low in the hierarchy will still give great benefit, however, when compared to the starting point before fermentation. Work within your ability to access the best ingredients.

What you will need:

Glass containers (I use litre size jugs or other glass jars)

Thin cotton or muslin cloths and an elastic band

Plastic measuring spoons

Plastic strainer/sieve

Liquid to culture: Dairy Milk (can be cow, goat sheep), coconut milk, any nut/seed milk, fresh soy milk, or (depending on grains) coconut water, fruit juice (I prefer fresh) or water with sugar added.

Plastic measuring jug

Glass jar (to store grains)

Ratio

1-2tbs grains: 1 litre liquid.

This is what works for me but everyone seems to have different proportions. I store my grains in the fridge when I am not using them but I try to have my milk/water at room temp before making it. **Be careful about temperature extremes**.

Directions:

Add liquid to ferment into a litre sized glass jar
(Always leave at least 2 cm space at the top)
Add milk/water grains with plastic measuring spoon
(Avoid metal as it reacts with the grains. Use only plastic and glass).
If you have very alkaline water, consider adding juice of a ¼ lemon/ 1 tbs of ready made kefir
Cover top with cloth and secure with a rubber band.
Leave in a warm place for 24-48 hours
(or as little as 12 hours sometimes in the summer)
Taste your Kefir and see if you like it.
Strain grains with plastic strainer

Use the plastic measuring spoon to move the grains to a clean glass jar. It's okay if there is a little starting liquid remaining. You only need to rinse the grains periodically (or if you are not going to use the grains for a while). This can be done in plain filtered water or water with a little baking soda. The picture on the left above is of the milk grains and the picture on the right is of grains strained from coconut water.

Store your excess/strained grains in a jar (called your 'grain hotel') and the resulting Kefir in the fridge. Fermentation is a method of preserving so your Kefir will preserved in the fridge for a long time. Use your sense of smell and taste before consuming the product, If in doubt there is no problem with pouring it down the sink.

I ferment to taste. If the Kefir is too sour, reduce either the amount of grains or the amount of time left to ferment. If the Kefir takes longer to ferment increase the amount of grains, decrease the amount of liquid you are fermenting, increase the temperature with a heating pad, or place on top of the fridge. Find what works for you and your environment. This may change as the seasons change.

Stir periodically (especially in the case of coconut milk and almond milk which naturally separates). Milk will taste sour and 'off' and even a little cheesy. The water will smell yeasty and may get a little fizzy.

As the grains live off the sugar during the culturing process, the shorter the time you allow to culture, the sweeter the Kefir will be. The more you agitate the grains the thicker the mixture will become.

When you are happy, shake the grains vigorously then strain the grains through a plastic sieve. It's okay if some grains escape into the liquid. It just adds to the mix! You may also have more grains than when you started. You strain the grains in order to have grains to start a new batch.

I usually reserve at least a tablespoon of grains in order to start a new batch of Kefir but if you don't need to do this, it is safe to consume all the grains. If you find you have a lot of grains, you can either use some of the recipes in the books that include grains or share your grains with others.

This is the first fermentation. The following recipes are either directions for a second fermentation or for mixtures with the first fermentation product.

The Russian Method

The Russian method uses a series of two fermentations. It is easier to regulate the outcome using these two methods and is a way of making a large amount of Kefir without using grains.

You make the first batch of Kefir using the grains incubated in milk as described in the previous chapter. Once the grains have been strained you then use this liquid as the 'mother culture' (like with yoghurt starter). You can then add 1-3% of the vessel with mother culture and fresh milk. Leave to ferment again in about half the time. You no longer need to strain this Kefir before consumption.

I sometimes use this method when I am making continuous batches. There will be some Kefir left on the sides and at the bottom of the jug. I use this as the mother culture. I then pour in fresh milk, without rinsing out the jug and leave to ferment overnight. I do not need to strain again.

This can be a quicker way to make Kefir with the same benefits. It was also the original way Kefir was made in Russia.

Grain Maintenance

The grains are pretty hardy, so storing them in the fridge is generally fine. Some people however do experience some grain 'die off' or find that their grains are slow to multiply or ferment. I generally follow these guidelines:

Feed the grains by adding more sugar and better quality ingredients (i.e. fresh milk rather than pasteurised).

Rotate whatever liquid you are fermenting (thus effectively rinsing the grains).

Rinse the grains by adding them to water (or water with baking soda) for a few hours before straining. This is especially useful if your Kefir is developing a strong sulfur smell.

It is also worthwhile experimenting with the use of an egg shell, mineral drops or molasses which may enrich the nutrient value of your water.

Always try to keep a tablespoon of grains aside to restart your fermenting if something goes wrong. These can also be stored in the freezer to keep them dormant.

Add some water grains to your milk grains every now and then to boost the grain consistency.

Store your grains in different jars to balance rotation and allow rest time for them (especially if your water Kefir starts to smell like sulphur. (Although still safe to drink I tend to use these batches for hair washing.)

The climate can alter the texture of your grains and affect how much they replicate. Humidity, temperature and altitude can all affect the way your grains operate. Be mindful of any changes in the environment when assessing the health of your grains.

Kefir likes a little acidity, so you may wish to add a little lemon juice (about 1 tbs for a litre of Kefir) or some ready made Kefir to help the grains if they seem to need a boost.

> # Chapter 2
> # KEFIR RECIPES

Drinks

Lychee Coconut Water Kefir

INGREDIENTS

2 cups/1 litre coconut water Kefir

A handful (5-6) peeled and stoned fresh lychees (you can use canned ones if necessary)

DIRECTIONS

Add the Lychees to the strained coconut water Kefir, cover and leave for a further 12-24 hours. You get a beautiful tart, sweet/sour, sharp and naturally sparkling Kefir. Strain out the Lychees. (You can eat the fruit on its own or in Coconut Yoghurt or a Green Kefir Smoothie or SCOBY Shake).

Drink straight, diluted with a little sparkling water or use in:

Green Kefir Smoothie, Watermelon Coconut Water Kefir, Morning Smoothie

(This also makes a mean cocktail with the addition of a little vodka or white rum)

Apple Water Kefir

INGREDIENTS

2 cups/1 litre of water Kefir
4-6 slices dehydrated apple, 1-2 tbsp apple sauce or fresh apple
(half an apple cored and peeled)

DIRECTIONS

Add the apples to the strained water Kefir, cover and leave for a further 12-24 hours. The concentrated sugar in the dehydrated apples should be sufficient. If you are using a fresh apple you may need to add extra sugar. Ferment to taste. Strain out the Apples. (Eat the fruit on its own or in Coconut Yoghurt or Green Kefir Smoothie or SCOBY Shake).

....

Drink straight, diluted with a little sparkling water or use in:

Green Kefir Smoothie, Digestive Calm Smoothie, or Carrot and Apple Water Kefir Juice,

Morning Smoothie

and

Camomile Tea, Raw Honey and Apple Water Kefir 'shampoo'

Mango Coconut Water Kefir

INGREDIENTS

2 cups/1 litre coconut water Kefir
4-6 slices dehydrated mango or fresh mango (half peeled and cubed)

DIRECTIONS

Add the mango to the strained water Kefir and cover and leave for a further 12-24 hours. You will get a really fruity, sharp and naturally sparkling Kefir. Strain out the mangos. (Eat the fruit on its own or in Coconut Yoghurt or Green Kefir Smoothie or SCOBY Shake).

....

Drink straight, diluted with a little sparkling water or use in:

Green Kefir Smoothie, Watermelon Coconut Water Kefir, Morning Smoothie

Clementine & Cinnamon Water Kefir

INGREDIENTS

2 cups/1 litre water Kefir
1-2 clementines/satsumas
pinch of cinnamon

DIRECTIONS

Add the clementines (peeled and segmented) and cinnamon to the strained water Kefir and cover and leave for a further 12-24 hours. You will get a really zesty, warming and naturally sparkling Kefir. Strain out the clementines. (Eat the fruit on its own or in Coconut Yoghurt or Green Kefir Smoothie or SCOBY Shake).

Drink straight, diluted with a little sparkling water or use in:

Green Kefir Smoothie

Mixed Berry Water Kefir

INGREDIENTS

2 cups/1 litre of water Kefir
Good handful of either fresh, dehydrated or frozen berries
(Can include blueberries, blackberries, strawberries, mulberries or cranberries)

DIRECTIONS

Add the mixed berries to the strained water Kefir, cover and leave for a further 12-24 hours. The sugar in the berries themselves will allow the Kefir to continue to ferment. Ferment to taste. Strain out the berries or they can also be left in to deepen the flavour in the fridge. (Eat the fruit on its own or in Coconut Yoghurt or Green Kefir Smoothie or SCOBY Shake).

Drink straight, diluted with a little sparkling water or use in:

Green Kefir Smoothie, Liver Support Smoothie, Morning Smoothie

Cacao & Vanilla Water Kefir

INGREDIENTS

2 cups/1 litre of water Kefir
(maple syrup water Kefir works the best for this recipe)
1-2 tbsp cacao nibs
1 tbsp dried cranberries
Vanilla essence

DIRECTIONS

When making the water/coconut water Kefir allow to ferment for less time to retain some of the sweetness from the sugar. Add Cacao nibs and vanilla to strained Water Kefir, cover and leave for a further 12-24 hours. You may need to add more sugar. Ferment to taste. Strain out the cacao nibs and they can be used in Green Kefir Smoothie or SCOBY Shake.

. . . .

Drink straight or diluted with a little sparkling water.

Lemon, Honey, Turmeric & Ginger Water Kefir

INGREDIENTS

2 cups/1 litre of water Kefir
4-6 slices of fresh ginger
4-6 slices of fresh turmeric root or ½ tsp dried turmeric
The juice of 1 lemon
1 tbs raw honey

DIRECTIONS

Add the ginger, lemon and honey to the strained water Kefir, cover and leave for a further 12-24 hours.. Ferment to taste. The extra honey may mean the Kefir needs to ferment for longer. Strain out the ginger if desired. (You could also add star annise or cinnamon to this ferment for an extra immune boost.)

....

Drink straight, diluted with a little sparkling water or use in:

Green Kefir Smoothie, Digestive Calm Smoothie, or Scoby Shake

Culture Your Life
Kefir and Kombucha For Every Day Nourishment

Sunshine Shot

INGREDIENTS

4-6 slices of fermented ginger and turmeric from
Ginger, Lemon, Turmeric and Honey Water Kefir
1 cup of coconut water Kefir

DIRECTIONS

Add both ingredients to the blender and whizz together. This drink gives you an amazing boost to your immune system and really wakes you up in the morning! Drink straight away and in one go.

Beetroot, Carrot & Apple Water Kefir

INGREDIENTS

2 Cups/1 litre of water Kefir
1 small raw beetroot (peeled and sliced)
1 raw carrot (peeled and sliced)
1 apple (dehydrated, Apple Sauce, or fresh sliced apple)

DIRECTIONS

Add the beetroot, carrot and apple to the strained water Kefir, cover and leave for a further 12-24 hours. Ferment to taste. Strain out the beetroot, apple and ginger or they can be left in to deepen the flavour in the fridge. (Use the vegetables in your Green Kefir Smoothie.)

....

Drink straight, diluted with a little sparkling water or use in:

Green Kefir Smoothie, Digestive Calm Smoothie, or Scoby Shake

Pumpkin Pie Water Kefir

INGREDIENTS

2 Cups/1 litre water Kefir
1-2 tbsp pumpkin puree
Pinch of pumpkin pie spice
Dash of maple syrup (optional)

DIRECTIONS

Add the pumpkin puree to the strained water kefir and the pinch of pumpkin pie mix. Leave to ferment for a further 12-24 hours. If you wish, this does not need to be strained, although it may need to be stirred before drinking.

....

Drink straight, diluted with a little sparkling water or use in:

Green Kefir Smoothie or Scoby Shake

Blueberry and Vanilla

INGREDIENTS

2 Cups/1 litre of water Kefir/coconut water Kefir
1-2 tbsp blueberries (fresh or frozen)
Vanilla essence

DIRECTIONS

Add the blueberries and vanilla to the strained water Kefir, cover and leave for a further 12-24 hours.. Ferment to taste. Strain out the blueberries.

Drink straight, diluted with a little sparkling water or use in;

Green Kefir Smoothie or Scoby Shake

Cucumber and Mint

INGREDIENTS

2 Cups/1 litre of water Kefir/coconut Water Kefir
1-2 tbsp cucumber (Peeled and sliced)
1tbs fresh chopped mint or mint essence

DIRECTIONS

Add the cucumber and mint to the strained water Kefir, cover and leave for a further 12-24 hours.. Ferment to taste. Strain out the cucumber and mint and add to smoothie.

Drink straight, diluted with a little sparkling water or use in;

....

Green Kefir Smoothie, Digestive Calm Smoothie, or Scoby Shake

Apple & Fig Water Kefir

INGREDIENTS

2 cups/ 1 ltre water Kefir
2 tbsp Apple Sauce or 3-4 slices of dehydrated apple
1-2 dried/dehydrated figs

DIRECTIONS

Add apple and figs to strained water Kefir and leave to ferment for 12-24 hours. Strain out the figs. Stir or shake before drinking.

....

Drink straight, diluted with a little sparkling water or use in;

Green Kefir Smoothie, Digestive Calm Smoothie, or Scoby Shake

Culture Your Life
Kefir and Kombucha For Every Day Nourishment

Pomello Water Kefir

INGREDIENTS

2 cups/1 litre of water Kefir
(Made from maple syrup/coconut nectar or coconut sugar)
½ pomello (peeled with pith removed)

DIRECTIONS

Add the Pomello to the strained Water Kefir, cover and leave for a further 12-24 hours. Ferment to taste. Strain out the pomelo. (use the fruit in your Green Kefir Smoothie)

....

Drink straight, diluted with a little sparkling water or use in;

Green Kefir Smoothie, Digestive Calm Smoothie, or Scoby Shake

Culture Your Life
Kefir and Kombucha For Every Day Nourishment

Kefir Milkshake
(Chocolate, Strawberry and Banana flavours)

Serves 2-3

INGREDIENTS

1 cups milk Kefir (nut/seed, dairy, coconut or oat)
1 cup of milk (nut/seed, dairy, coconut or oat)
½ cup frozen Coconut Yoghurt
2 drops of vanilla essence
½ tbsp maple syrup/raw honey/coconut nectar (optional)
½ cup of ice (optional)
This is the base mixture. You can then add any flavouring you like.

Strawberry
Add 5-10 fresh or frozen strawberries
Strawberry Coconut Yoghurt or Strawberry Kefir Ice-cream

Chocolate
Add 1 tbsp raw cacao powder
½ tsp cinnamon

Banana
1 banana
2 drops banana essence (optional)
½ tsp cinnamon

DIRECTIONS

Add all ingredients to a blender (a high speed one is ideal but not necessary). Blend until smooth.

Banana Bread Kefir

Serves 2-3

INGREDIENTS

2 cups of dairy Kefir
(You can use Kefir made from other milks or coconut water Kefir with a similar effect, but the thickness of the dairy milk Kefir works well.)
½ cup of coconut milk
1 banana
1 tbs almond meal, or soaked oats or frozen/fresh Coconut Yoghurt
3 drops of banana essence
3 drops vanilla essence
½ tsp cinnamon
½ tsp nutmeg
Pinch of pink Himalayan salt
½ tsp raw honey or maple syrup

DIRECTIONS

Blend until the banana is smooth and creamy. This smoothie is inspired by my love of Banana bread- see Almond Kefir Banana Muffins

....

(Also makes a mean cocktail with the addition of a little Dark Rum)

Morning Smoothie

Serves 2-3

INGREDIENTS

2 cups oat or coconut Milk
1 banana
1tsp chia seeds
1tsp hemp seeds
1 cup coconut water Kefir (Can use any Kefir or flavoured Kefir recipe)
1 tbs coconut butter
1 tbsp nut butter (not not use if giving to children under 1)
1/2 tsp cinnamon

DIRECTIONS

Add all ingredients to a blender (a high speed one is ideal but not necessary). Blend until smooth.

I like to get as much nutrition into my kids as possible. I also like to give them - and myself - a really good start to the day. We have this alongside our breakfast or as a mid afternoon snack. It is also a great snack for pregnant and breastfeeding mums. I have used oat and coconut milk to keep it safe for weaning babies from 6 months upwards. Otherwise, any milk (nut and seed) and or milk Kefir can be used.

Dreamy Almond

Serves 2-3

INGREDIENTS

1 cup almond milk
½ cup almond milk Kefir
2 tbsp almond meal
2 drops vanilla essence
2 drops almond essence
1/2 avocado, banana or coconut meat
1 tbsp coconut oil
½ tsp cinnamon (optional)
1 tsp honey or maple syrup (optional)

DIRECTIONS

Add all ingredients to a blender (a high speed one is ideal but not necessary). Blend until smooth. Sweeten with raw honey or maple syrup if necessary.

I was inspired to make this recipe by the packaged almond milk of a similar name. I have tried to pack this one full of nutrients and flavour. It is a really filling protein and fat laden smoothie which makes it a perfect post workout snack or a great snack for pregnant, breastfeeding moms, growing kids and teenagers!

Chocolate Avocado Pudding Kefirshake

Serves 2-3

INGREDIENTS

1 cup milk Kefir
1 cup milk (dairy, nut, oat or coconut)
1-2 Chocolate Avocado Pudding ice cubes
1 banana
1 tbs almond meal or unflavoured good quality protein powder
2 drops of vanilla essence
½ tsp cinnamon (optional)
1 tsp honey or maple syrup (optional)

DIRECTIONS

Add all ingredients to a blender (a high speed one is ideal but not necessary). Blend until smooth

Whenever I make Chocolate Avocado pudding I always put some in small cupcake cases and store in the freezer to rather make into ice-cream or this alternative morning smoothie.

This recipe can be made with dairy, almond or coconut milk Kefir or a mixture.

Watermelon Cooler

Serves 1-2

INGREDIENTS

1 cup coconut water Kefir
1/2 cup watermelon juice (2 slices of watermelon blended with a little water)

DIRECTIONS

Add all ingredients to a blender (a high speed one is ideal but not necessary). Blend until smooth.

....

The taste is sweet and tart and very refreshing. Adding ice to the blender will add a 'slushie' feel to it. This one is a big favourite of mine. Adding a teaspoon of basil seeds or chia seeds before drinking is nice too.

(Also makes a mean cocktail with the addition of a little vodka)

Carrot with Apple Water Kefir

Serves 2-3

INGREDIENTS

1 carrot (or carrot juice if not using a high speed blender)
1 ½ cups Apple Water Kefir (or other flavoured Kefirs)
Optional: small piece of ginger

DIRECTIONS

Add all ingredients to a blender (a high speed one is ideal but not necessary). Blend until smooth

Green Kefir Smoothie

Serves 1-2

INGREDIENTS

1 ½ cups coconut water Kefir (or other flavoured Kefir)

1 cup greens

(you can use pea shoots, spinach, sweet potato leaves, kale, frozen peas, lettuce or a mix of them all)

1-2 celery sticks

1 mini cucumber

¼ cup fresh herbs

(Oregano, mint or basil work well or a combination)

Optional Extras;

Fermented fruit from other recipes

Mango, watermelon, papaya, pear, apple, berries, pomello, carrot or a combination

1 tbsp powdered greens (organic is preferable)

Chia or hemp seeds

Handful of ice cubes

DIRECTIONS

Blend with a high speed blender.

Serves 1-2

INGREDIENTS

½ cup almond milk Kefir or coconut water kefir (or Mixed Berry Water Kefir/Cacao and Vanilla Water Kefir)
1 cups almond or oat milk
½ tbsp sesame seeds
1 tbsp milk thistle seeds
1 tsp powdered greens (organic is preferable)
1 tbsp flax oil
½ tbsp coconut oil
1 banana (or fermented fruit from other recipes)
1 tsp raw honey (optional)
1 tbsp maca (optional)

DIRECTIONS

Add all the ingredients to a blender (a high speed one is ideal but not necessary). Blend until smooth. If you do not have a high speed blender it will be easier (and less gritty) to use a coffee grinder to grind Milk Thistle and sesame seeds first.

Liver Green Kefir Smoothie

Coconut Water Kefir Rehydration Drink

Serves 1
INGREDIENTS

½ cup coconut water Kefir or Watermelon with Coconut Water Kefir
½ cup coconut water or filtered water
½ tsp powdered greens
1 tbsp chia

DIRECTIONS

Add all the ingredients to your glass and stir vigorously. Drink quickly or keep stirring.

I recently started using this drink post exercise (I always take a shot of Kefir, normally a flavoured water Kefir, before exercise). It seems that these ingredients may help the body to replace electrolytes (the bacteria in the Kefir help to make the minerals from the coconut water more bio available). Certainly it seems to help create energy and it also contains important antioxidants, fats and proteins (in the Chia). I find that I can run faster, and for longer, I feel stronger and I also recover faster. I love it!

Food

Garlic Kefir Dip

INGREDIENTS

1 cup milk Kefir
2-3 cloves of garlic (can be roasted for a sweeter taste)
¾ cup spring onions
pinch salt
pinch black pepper
pinch paprika
pinch cumin
½ tsp coconut sugar (optional)

DIRECTIONS

Add all ingredients to the food processor and whizz till garlic is all minced in. Stir in spring onions.

This dip is really good with chips (fries and crisps). It is also nice poured over meatballs or falafel, or used in fajitas or vegetarian/meat burgers. It is great at barbeques on top of baked potatoes or over sweet-corn and it can also be used as a delicious and simple dressing over greens, in coleslaw, with couscous or potato or quinoa salads. Very versatile!

Kefir Cucumber Ranch Dressing

INGREDIENTS

1/2 tsp chopped/dried parsley
1/2 tsp chopped/dried chives
1 tsp garlic powder/1 roasted garlic clove
1 tsp lemon juice (1/2 lemon)
1/4 tsp pink Himalayan salt and pepper to season
1-2 cups dairy Kefir
1tsp coconut sugar (optional)
1 cucumber peeled and finely diced

DIRECTIONS

Add all the ingredients in a bowl and mix well. Season with salt/pepper/sugar to taste

Optional: add some finely grated chedder cheese/ Kefir Cheese.

....

Serve as a dip or salad dressing.

Kefir Cheese

INGREDIENTS

1 litre of dairy milk Kefir (made from un-homogenised/raw milk works better)
1 nut bag
1 bowl
1 chopstick

DIRECTIONS

First, make the milk Kefir (best left for 24 hours until nice and thick). If you need to strain off some grains do so by spooning some mixture off of the top. Then put all of the liquid into the nut-bag. Do not squeeze too much. Twist the top of the nut-bag and then wrap the excess material at the top of the bag around the chopstick, so that you can suspend the nut-bag over the jar or bowl (see pictures below). Leave for another 12-24 hours. There should be a clear, yellow Whey in the jar and cheese curds in the nut bag. Empty the curds out of the bag into a bowl.

FLAVOURING;

Season with a pinch of salt and pepper
You can add anything now:
Dried fruit such as cranberries, apricots, figs or blueberries
Chopped herbs (fresh or dried)
Maple Syrup and Cinnamon or **Lemon and Coconut** for a delicious Cream cheese frosting.

Lemon Kefir Cheese Cake

INGREDIENTS

400g ricotta cheese (you could also use coconut cream for dairy free)
200g kefir cheese
100g whipped cream
50g coconut sugar icing sugar
Juice of 2 lemons and the zest of one (or you can also use 2 tbs lemon curd)
Vanilla
Grated chocolate for the top
3 tsp gelatin in warm water (enough to dissolve the gelatin)
For the base
1 cup almonds/cashews
1 cup pecans
1 tbsp coconut oil
1 tbsp ghee (or nut butter)
1/2 tsp pink salt
5 medjool dates (pitted)

DIRECTIONS

Make the base by adding all the ingredients into the food processor. When combined, take out and press into a spring form pan lined with baking paper. Place in fridge to set.

Add the cheese, sugar, lemon, gelatin and vanilla together in a mixer and use the balloon whisk to whip together.

Fold in the whipped cream.

Pour onto the base and place in the fridge for 4 hours before serving.

Kefir Meat Jerky

INGREDIENTS

500g of sliced beef (I used the hot pot beef but you can use any cut (grass fed organic is ideal) and slice really thinly)
1 tbsp liquid aminos or coconut aminos
1/4 cup of apple cider vinegar/ Kombucha
1/4 cup of water Kefir (flavoured or not. I use coconut sugar to make my water kefir)
1tsp grated fresh ginger root
3 cloves of garlic crushed
Juice of half a lemon
1tsp mustard (I use Dijon)
1tbsp Apple Sauce (optional)
1 1/2 tbsp coconut sugar
pinch black pepper
Other optional extras:
Fennel seeds, cloves, cinnamon, coriander seeds, cumin

DIRECTIONS

Prepare the marinade by mixing all the ingredients together in a bowl. Keep the meat separate at first.

Taste the marinade and adjust if necessary.

Add the meat and cover. Allow the meat to marinade for between 10-24 hours.

Use baking paper and coconut oil to rub the sheets to try and reduce sticking (in the way you would grease a baking pan).

Cut the strips into bite size pieces and add to the dehydrator sheets

Dehydrate at 113 Fahrenheit or 45 degrees Centigrade. This is to keep the probiotic quality of the apple cider vinegar and Kefir. (You can also do it in your oven on the lowest setting for 6-12 hours) at for between 12 and 24 hours until the desired crispyness. This last sentence needs reworking; not clear.   Flip the jerky if necessary.

Store in an airtight container to retain freshness. Does not need to be kept in the fridge.

Kefir Soda Bread

My husband is Irish and the Irish love their bread. He has embraced being Gluten free for the most part and really enjoys making this bread:

INGREDIENTS

1 cup all purpose gluten free flour/oat flour,
1/2 cup buckwheat flour
1/2 cup almond flour
30g steel cut oats (or normal oats if you are not celiac) optional,
1/2 tsp salt,
1tbsp honey/coconut nectar/maple syrup
1tsp baking powder,
1-2 cup milk Kefir (dairy or nut).

DIRECTIONS

Soak your flour in the Kefir overnight.

Preheat oven to 200 degrees C. Add dry ingredients into a bowl, then add wet ingredients. Try to mix as little as possible, place on grease proof paper on baking sheet, dust lightly with more all purpose flour and cut a deep cross in the top. Bake for 30 mins until brown on the outside!

As gluten free bread goes, this one has a nice consistency and is delicious spread thick with butter or Kefir Cheese.

Banana & Kefir Muffins

INGREDIENTS

3 bananas
2 eggs
4 tbsp coconut oil
1 tbsp coconut Butter
4 tbsp almond milk Kefir
2 tbsp raw honey/maple syrup/coconut nectar
3 drops banana essence
3 drops vanilla essence
1 cup gluten free biscuit and baking flour
1/2 cup almond meal (almond flour, ground almond)
2 tbsp buckwheat flour
1tsp baking powder
1/2 tsp pink Himalayan salt

OPTIONAL EXTRAS:

handful of raisins/dates
handful raw cacao nibs
chocolate chips (from Homemade Chocolate), sesame seeds
toasted coconut ,crushed nuts

DIRECTIONS

Heat the oven to 180 degrees C.

Mix wet ingredients together in a mixer with a K beater if possible.

Mix in the sifted, dry ingredients. Make sure you scrape down the sides to incorporate all of the mixture together.

Add in optional extras and mix through.

....

I like to use a mini muffin pan (as pictured), but this can be made in muffin cases or as a whole cake to be cut up. Cook for 20 mins or until cooked through and golden brown.

Nate's Blueberry & Kefir Mauffins

INGREDIENTS

2 cups buckwheat flour
¼ cup of coconut flour
1 tsp baking powder (Aluminium free)
1/2 cup of coconut sugar
1 pack (2 cups) frozen blueberries
2 cups of milk or nut milk Kefir (or Blueberry and Vanilla Water Kefir)
3/4 cup of coconut oil (melted if necessary)
3 eggs
(you can replace one of the eggs with 1tsp chia seeds + 3 tsp water for added nutrition)
2 drops vanilla essence

DIRECTIONS

Heat oven to 180 degrees C. Mix dry ingredients together (flour, baking powder and sugar). Fold in the blueberries. This may prevent the blueberries from dropping to the bottom.

Blueberry Flour

Whisk up the wet ingredients together (Kefir, eggs, vanilla) and add to the mix.

At first, when I wasn't used to making muffins, I got a dry clumpy mix (Buckwheat flour can suck up moisture!) so I added more Kefir. But then I found that the blueberries also added some moisture and they came out great.

....

I like to use a mini muffin pan, but this can be made in muffin cases or as a whole cake to be cut up. Cook for 20 mins or until cooked through and golden brown.

Kefir Pancakes

INGREDIENTS

3 eggs
1 mashed banana (optional)
½ cup of gluten free flour (all purpose)
2-3 tbsp almond meal
1 tbsp coconut flour

100mls dairy, oat or nut milk Kefir
1tsp baking powder (Aluminium Free)
2 pinches of salt
1 tsp coconut sugar (optional)

Optional extras;

Fruit: banana, mango, berries
Ground nuts, flax or seeds
Dehydrated fruits (cranberries, banana, apple, blueberries, mango or raisins)
Cacao nibs/chocolate chips (from Homemade Chocolate)
Or a combination

DIRECTIONS

I use my two mixer bowls for this. In one I place the egg whites and half of the salt. Use the balloon whisk and whisk until you have soft peaks. This step makes your pancakes really light and fluffy. In the other bowl I place the egg yolks, flour, baking powder, sugar, Kefir and remaining salt. Mix the ingredients in the second bowl well with a balloon whisk then fold in the egg whites and mashed banana (or other fruit). This is your base mix.

In a frying pan, add some butter or coconut oil and add the mixture with a spoon. As a family we like small round American style pancakes but this mixture will also make French style crepes. Add optional extras by sprinkling them gently on the top.

When bubbles appear, flip the pancake over and allow to cook for another couple of minutes! Repeat. Stack them up and take to the table!

Serve with your favourite toppings. We like Coconut yoghurt, Raw jam, nut butter, mixed fruit salad, bacon, or Maple syrup/coconut nectar. Delicious and nutritious!

Coconut Yoghurt

INGREDIENTS

1 cup of coconut meat
A drizzle to 1/2 cup of coconut water Kefir or any milk/water Kefir (depending on the wetness of the meat)

DIRECTIONS

Add the Coconut meat to a blender (a high speed one is ideal, but not necessary) or a food processor. Add a little Kefir to get the yoghurt started.

Blend on slow speed to start with and then on high, adding more Kefir as necessary until you reach a creamy consistency.

Add mix to small jars (or one big jar). This makes about 8 portions of yoghurt (with each portion being about 3 tbs).

Maintain the temperature at 100 degrees F and leave for 12 hours. I use my dehydrator but you can use a cool oven, a yoghurt maker, a warm part of the house (such as the top of the fridge) or you can wrap the jars in a towel. This also means that this is a raw yoghurt.

Then store in the fridge. Delicious. Below are some flavouring ideas

STRAWBERRY COCONUT YOGHURT;

Add 4 strawberries before blending. Follow recipe for coconut yoghurt. Or you can reblend the coconut yoghurt after the second fermentation with 4 strawberries for a sweeter yoghurt.

VANILLA AND CINNAMON;

Same as above. Add ½ a vanilla pod and ½ tsp cinnamon to the base mix either before or after the second fermentation.

Strawberry Kefir Ice Cream

INGREDIENTS

1 ½ cups of Strawberry Coconut yoghurt or Coconut Yoghurt
1 cup of fresh coconut milk (you could also use any nut, oat or dairy milk)
4-8 Strawberries preferably frozen or fresh then frozen
(You can also add the fermented berries from Mixed Berry Water Kefir)
3 drops Vanilla essence
1 tbsp honey or maple syrup (optional)

DIRECTIONS

Make the Coconut Yoghurt or use Coconut Cream (the same recipe but it uses coconut water rather than coconut Kefir and there is no need for a second fermentation).

Add fresh coconut milk, coconut oil, strawberries, vanilla essence and optional sweetener. Blend in a blender or food processor until smooth.

There are many ways to make ice cream. The colder the ingredients the quicker the ice-cream will set. You could use an ice-cream maker (in my case the ice-cream attachment to my mixer), you could put the ingredients in a bowl and stir/blend periodically (every 30 mins) to break up the ice crystals, or you could store the liquid in ice cube trays and then blend when frozen.

You can also add some soaked cashew nuts to the mix before blending to help to keep it soft and scoop-able! I like to keep mine nut free.

Rocky Road Kefir Ice Cream

INGREDIENTS

1 cup of coconut yoghurt
1 cup/236mls fresh coconut milk (you could also use any nut, oat or dairy milk)
1 banana (optional)
1-2 tbsp coconut oil
1 tbsp raw cacao powder
pinch of Himalayan pink salt
3 drops vanilla essence
1 tbsp honey or maple syrup (optional)
Rocky Road bits;
100g Homemade Chocolate
(Marshmallows, chopped nuts, chocolate chips, dried fruit, soaked seeds, toasted coconut…)

DIRECTIONS

Make the Coconut Yoghurt or use Coconut Cream (same recipe just without a second fermentation).

Add fresh coconut milk, coconut oil, cacao, salt, vanilla essence and optional sweetener. You can also add some soaked cashew nuts to the mix now, before blending to keep it soft and scoop-able.

Blend until smooth. Stir in mashed banana together with your choice and volume of rocky bits!

....

There are many ways to make ice cream. The colder the ingredients the quicker the ice-cream will set. You could use an ice-cream maker (in my case the ice-cream attachment to my mixer), you could put the ingredients in a bowl and stir/blend periodically (every 30 mins) to break up the ice crystals, or you could store the liquid in ice cube trays and then blend when frozen.

Mint Chocolate Chip Kefir Ice Cream

INGREDIENTS

1 cup/ 400g coconut meat
1/2 cup 200ml Coconut Yoghurt
1tbs milk/almond/coconut water Kefir
1-2 tbsp coconut oil
1 tbsp mint infused water
2 drops mint essence
1 tsp Coconut nectar
1/2 Cup 100g Homemade Chocolate with 2 drops mint essence
1 cup soaked cashew nuts (optional)

DIRECTIONS

Make the Coconut Yoghurt or use Coconut Cream (same recipe just without a second fermentation).

Add dairy, almond or coconut water Kefir, coconut oil and the rest of the ingredients to the blender. You can also add some soaked cashew nuts to the mix now, before blending, to keep it soft and scoop-able

Blend together all the ingredients except the homemade chocolate until smooth. This works well with frozen coconut meat. Cut up the chocolate and stir in.

There are many ways to make ice cream. The colder the ingredients the quicker the ice-cream will set. You could use an ice-cream maker (in my case the ice-cream attachment to my mixer), you could put the ingredients in a bowl and stir/blend periodically (every 30 mins) to break up the ice crystals, or you could store the liquid in ice cube trays and then blend when frozen. You can also freeze this in ice lolly molds.

Kefir Gummies

INGREDIENTS

1 cup of coconut water, any juice or fruit puree
6tbs gelatin
½ cup flavoured Kefir
½ cup Kombucha (optional you could do all Kefir or all Kombucha)
Drizzle of maple syrup (optional)

DIRECTIONS

Start by gently warming the coconut water or juice. Add gelatin slowly to avoid clumping. When it is cooled to lukewarm add Kefir and Kombucha. Sweeten to taste if necessary. Pour into molds and store in the fridge to set. Add fruit if desired.

Flavour ideas:

Ginger, Lemon, Turmeric and Honey water Kefir

Elderberry water Kefir with coconut water

Raspberry puree with Mixed Berry Water Kefir/milk Kefir (for raspberry and cream)

....

Serve with Kefir ice cream for a time old favourite- Jelly and Ice-cream!

Cosmetics

Why is Kefir so great for cosmetics?

Kefir has been used specifically as a beauty product, both internally and externally, for centuries. Cleopatra's famed milk baths would undoubtedly have been with fermented milk. But why does Kefir do such an amazing job of clearing and brightening the skin while retaining a youthful complexion?

Kefir milk contains alpha hydroxy acid (AHA) in the form of lactic acid. The active ingredients and the vitality of the bacteria within the Kefir make the nutrients far easier to absorb, whether through the skin or through the digestive system. This means that both drinking the Kefir and bathing, spritzing, cleansing with it (and even washing your hair with it) will all have beneficial effects. It is even reported that the lactic acids together with peptides (protein bonds) can also help lighten the skin and have a positive effect on acne and other skin conditions. This has not gone un-noticed in the cosmetic world with many well named brands bringing 'probiotic' skincare, deodorants, hand sanitisers and so on into the market.

Most natural 'antibacterials' (lavender, lemon, tea tree, garlic etc) are actually *natural balancers.* They naturally get to work on changing the ratio of bacteria (yeasts, molds and fungus). It may be surprising to realise but every single species has a very important role both inside and outside our body. Yes, even candida, listeria and helicobacter pylori serve a purpose.

I can report smoother skin and shinier hair. I have tried and tested all of these recipes to great effect on myself and my young children. It is very effective on sunburn and irritated skin and when used generally as a bi-weekly face mask. I have sensitive skin but if you experience any irritation, rash or upset then please discontinue use of the products.

Using Kefir internally and topically either as a spray or in bath water) has been seen to improve eczema and psoriasis conditions, both in children and adults alike. It is also safe to use on young babies.

The best way to ensure there is a balanced bacterial environment is to use your alive homemade ferments. Off the shelf products will have gone through so many processes to ensure product 'safety' which will compromise the natural ratios, bacterial component and by-products which are integral to its efficiency.

Hand Sanitiser

INGREDIENTS

1/2 bottle water
½ bottle water Kefir
(Depending on size of bottle)
5-10 drops of lavender
spray bottle

DIRECTIONS

Add all your ingredients to the spray bottle. Keep in your hand bag or by the sink and use instead of soap. Simply spray on hands and either allow to air dry or use a towel to dab dry.

Skin Soother

INGREDIENTS

1 tbsp to a cup of any Kefir (depending on how big and deep your bath is!)
Or the same amount of Kefir grains (milk or water)

DIRECTIONS

Use any Kefir (I like to use coconut water). You can also use excess grains. Add to a warm bath (too hot will kill the bacteria) and enjoy a skin softening and rejuvenating bath.

Bacteria are essential to good skin and body health, both on the outside as a first line of defence and to remove dead cells, and from the inside to help absorb key nutrients and eliminate toxins.

This is really great for any skin irritations including nappy rash, eczema, acne, dry skin and oily skin as the bacteria will repopulate the skin and help encourage new growth and repair from both outside and inside.

Sunburn Soother

INGREDIENTS

1 cup of Kefir (or excess grains)
5 drops of lavender
5 drops of calendula tincture
1 handful of epsom salts
4 drops of Bach Rescue Remedy

DIRECTIONS

Add to a warm bath (not too hot to ensure survival of the Kefir) and enjoy.

....

Any area that has seen too much sun can instantly be calmed down in the bath with the above mix. This can also be added to a spray bottle to apply directly to skin.

After Swim Skin Balancerr

INGREDIENTS

½ quantity water
½ quantity Water Kefir
1-2 drops of lavender and calendula
pinch of of epsom salts
Dash of coconut oil

DIRECTIONS

Add to a spray bottle.

Use directly after being in the sun/pool (can be kept in your beach or pool bag). This formula is great to help counter the effects of chemicals in a swimming pool and acts well as an after swim shampoo for kids and adults alike.

....

This is also good sprayed in your hair for defined curls and to de-frizz.

Kefir Face Mask

INGREDIENTS

1 tbs-1 cup of Kefir grains depending on where you are using the mask.
1 tsp-1 tbs coconut oil
Drizzle to 1 tsp raw honey.

DIRECTIONS

Mix the grains in a bowl with the coconut oil and honey or use it straight on the skin. Can also be kept in the fridge. This can be used on the face, neck and all over the body. It is also a great hair mask.

Leave for 15 mins to an hour. If irritation occurs, wash off.

Gently wash off with a face cloth. If using on the hair use Kefir shampoo to wash out the oil.

Kefir Grain Bath Salts/Body Scrub

bath or apply to the body in a circular motion onto dry skin and then get into a bath or shower off. The grains themselves (water or milk) can also be used directly on the skin as a good body scrub.

INGREDIENTS

1 cup of epsom salts
½ cup of sea salt of pink himalayan salt
1 tbsp coconut oil
½ tbsp kefir grains
Essential oils of your choice
Blends I like:
10 drops lemon oil
10 drops orange oil
5 drops ginger oil
or
10 drops lavender oil

5 drops frankinsence oil
5 drops of vanilla essence

Mix the ingredients together in a jar and either store in the fridge or in a cool dry place. Use when desired.
If you are unsure about using essential oils please ask your aromatherapist.

Culture Your Life
Kefir and Kombucha For Every Day Nourishment

Coconut Water Kefir Hair Rinse

INGREDIENTS

1 ½ cups of coconut water Kefir
1 ½ cups of water

DIRECTIONS

Use 1/3 of the mixture every day as an alternative to shampoo. Pour over hair, Leave in hair for 5-10 mins and rinse out. It can also be used after shampooing as a rinse. Can also be put in an empty spray bottle and sprayed on the ends of the hair before the shower.

Please note: when you first give up conventional shampoos your hair can go through a 'detox'. It may get greasy, dry and even change colour slightly (all this happened to me). You may also get an itchy scalp. Keep going with it, however, as things will eventually regulate as the chemically treated hair grows out and thicker, shinier hair grows in its place. How long this takes will depend on the length of your hair. If this is not conducive to your lifestyle, then just use these recipes as a rinse after your normal hair routine or alternate with your regular products until you are comfortable.

Rosemary Tea, Water Kefir & Raw Honey hair rinse

(Good for dark hair)

INGREDIENTS

1 cup rosemary tea (fresh or dried rosemary infused in boiling water and left to cool)
1 cup of water Kefir or coconut water Kefir
1 tbsp honey
1 tbsp of apple cider vinegar

DIRECTIONS

Use 1/3 of the mixture every day as an alternative to shampooing. Pour over hair, leave in hair for 5-10 mins and rinse out. It can also be used after shampooing as a rinse. Can also be put in an empty spray bottle and sprayed on the ends of the hair before the shower.

Please note: when you first give up conventional shampoos your hair can go through a 'detox'. It may get greasy, dry and even change colour slightly (all this happened to me). You may also get an itchy scalp. Keep going with it, however, as things will eventually regulate as the chemically treated hair grows out and thicker, shinier hair grows in its place. How long this takes will depend on the length of your hair. If this is not conducive to your lifestyle, then just use these recipes as a rinse after your normal hair routine or alternate with your regular products until you are comfortable.

Chamomile Tea, Raw Honey and Apple Water Kefir Rinse

(Good for Fair Hair)

INGREDIENTS

1 cup of camomile tea (dried camomile flowers or tea bags infused in boiling water and left to cool)
1 cup of Apple Water Kefir
2 drops of vanilla essence
1tsp raw honey and
1 tbs of apple cider vinegar

DIRECTIONS

Use 1/3 of the mixture every day as an alternative to shampoo. Pour over hair, leave in hair for 5-10 mins and rinse out. It can also be used after shampooing as a rinse. Can also be put in an empty spray bottle and sprayed on the ends of the hair before the shower.

Please note: when you first give up conventional shampoos your hair can go through a 'detox'. It may get greasy, dry and even change colour slightly (all this happened to me). You may also get an itchy scalp. Keep going with it, however, as things will eventually regulate as the chemically treated hair grows out and thicker, shinier hair grows in its place. How long this takes will depend on the length of your hair. If this is not conducive to your lifestyle, then just use these recipes as a rinse after your normal hair routine or alternate with your regular products until you are comfortable.

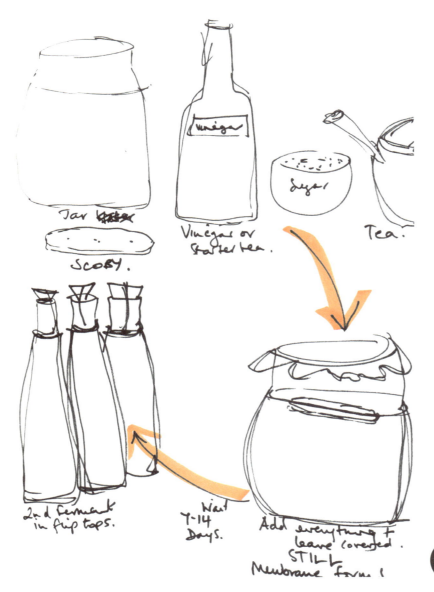

Chapter 3
KOMBUCHA

What is Kombucha

 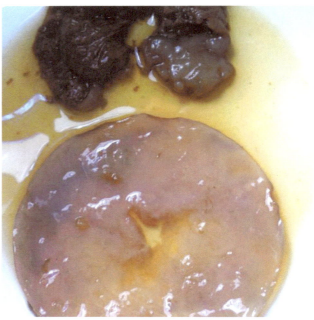

Kombucha is a fermented tea, also known as Tea Fungus (C. Dufresne, (2000)) which is thought to have originated in either China or Russia. An incredibly delicious, refreshing and tart drink, which after fermentation is slightly sparkling. It is a lot like apple cider in its benefits and taste. Kombucha, like Kefir, contains a tiny amount of alcohol. As a drink Kombucha is very low in sugar (the bacteria consume it), full of the antioxidant benefits found in tea, simple to make, and full of health giving properties.

The drink is made with a SCOBY (Symbiotic Colony Of Bacteria and Yeast), known as 'The Mother'. The Scoby is a bit like a disc which is created from a membrane forming on the surface of a liquid as it ferments (see pictures above).

To make it you simply need:

Tea (black, green or white),
a SCOBY,
some brewed Kombucha (or vinegar for an acidic environment),
filtered water and sugar.

That and a glass jar and some time.

Kombucha fermentation is an aerobic process so it has to float (the surface is where the oxygen is in its highest concentration). It is best to use a wide glass vessel (no metal should be used in brewing Kombucha or Kefir) that is partially filled. Your SCOBY will generate a membrane that is the same size and shape as your vessel. As you make more Kombucha with the same SCOBY, the SCOBY will get thicker and generally grow in layers that you can peel off and use to generate other batches and share (SCOBY Babies). As there is no added benefit in having a thicker SCOBY it is good to give them away to others. Some additional ways to use the SCOBYs are also included in the recipes in this book.

"Bubble Bubble - Toil and Trouble"

- Kombucha has been consumed for over 2000 years and is said to be **Magical!**

www.loulanatural.com

Health Benefits of Kombucha

Kombucha's health benefits have been shouted from the rooftops by many. The claims are numerous and pretty broad and varied in nature, from digestive enhancement to helping to reverse some cancer cell growth. For example it is claimed that Kombucha contains Glucoric Acid (which is a liver support and may aid in the elimination of toxins) although many discredit this. Each batch will be slightly different in makeup and in what it contains and this makes it very difficult to control research and substantiate any claims. Most of the claims seem to relate to the tea's own health giving properties and the way in which the fermentation process opens up the bio-availability of these properties (C. Dufresne, (2000)). As yet, it seems that most claims rely on anecdotal evidence but Kombucha is enjoying a massive revival in the US and many products can be bought straight off the shelf.

Despite the lack of scientific evidence, however, it is generally accepted that Kombucha offers great health benefits in that it acts as a general 'tonic'. Much like Kefir, Kombucha's probiotic nature acts as a stimulant and regulator to the immune system. It also shares a similar yeast and bacterial profile to Kefir. Again, the nutritional constituents will rely on the quality and nutritional value of what you are fermenting - in this case black tea, green tea and white tea. As in Kefir, organic starting points are preferred, although not essential. 'The Mother' in Kombucha also greatly resembles the 'mother' found in the production of apple cider vinegar and many claim its organism make-up is exactly the same. For this reason, you often see similar benefits claimed for Kombucha as for apple cider vinegar.

Since Kombucha is also sold as a commercial product it is necessary in the US to carry health warnings. With differences occurring in each batch, making research very difficult, it is tricky for the FDA to approve any claims relating to health benefits, hence the health warnings. From my personal experience I have felt beneficial effects from taking Kombucha. After drinking it the first few times I experienced a gentle purging of my digestive system and I soon learnt to take it at intervals, and in small doses. Over time I have been able to rebalance and heal my digestive and liver function and am now able to enjoy it on a daily basis without any repercussions. Many other clients, friends and even my husband have not felt any 'ill-effects', just the benefits of the refreshing vitality it contains. This leads me to agree with the idea that Kombucha may have a role in gently supporting and stimulating the liver. If you feel a response from the body after taking Kombucha, I would suggest that this may be seen as a good thing. It may even highlight that the body has a need for the benefits being supplied.

I find it amazing that the ritual of brewing Kombucha tea has been in existence for centuries (and in less sanitised kitchens and conditions through the ages too). As an 'alive' product I believe it can only help us to re-populate the beneficial bacteria that we need and thus provide support for our health. But as with all products claiming to be 'miracle cure-all's' look at who is making the claim (whether for or against) and see what they have to gain. Better to try it for yourself and see how your body feels and reacts.

From left: The Sugars to be used for Kombucha, Coconut sugar, coconut nectar and maple syrup. The teas used in my Kombucha recipes (clockwise Jasmine, black tea, white Tea and green tea)

5 Reasons to Brew Kombucha

1. Kombucha is simple to make and requires common ingredients that you would find at home (tea, sugar and vinegar). It can be made in any size jar. It normally takes between 7-14 days for the first fermentation to be completed, so once you brew it all you need is a little patience. Add anything you like to the Second Fermentation and again simply leave for another 7-14 days. Kombucha can be brewed to taste. The longer you leave it, the more sour and vinegar-like it becomes. It can also be diluted to taste (normally with soda water) as it is very strong in flavour, high in acid and very potent as a digestive aid and liver cleanser.

2. Drinking Kombucha can often have very positive side effects, mainly in clearing and aiding the digestive system (diarrhea), cleansing the liver and supporting the elimination of toxins. However you may also experience headaches, muscle spasms and a flare up of skin conditions and other inflammatory conditions - all signs that the body may be clearing toxins and be in the process of healing. As your body comes back to balance it is worth starting slowly with Kombucha and checking in with how you are feeling every time you drink it.

3. Kombucha is rich in many good probiotic strains and these will take up residence in your digestive system and rebalance the bacteria in your body. Kombucha also contains many healthy acids, which all have health giving benefits, in the same way that apple cider vinegar does. By providing both probiotic and essential acids, combined with the antioxidants in the tea, and other vitamins and minerals contained in the sugar and the SCOBY itself, Kombucha becomes a very powerful supplement for health and vitality.

4. Kombucha drinkers have reported a reduction in many symptoms, especially arthritic pain, IBS symptoms and allergy reactions. At the same time, many people have reported balanced ph levels and increased metabolic rate leading to more energy, a decrease in sugar cravings, reduced headaches and migraines, improved skin conditions and a reduction in candida overgrowth symptoms. In some cases, the symptoms of many more chronic conditions have also been alleviated and it has even been reported that Kombucha may have helped to return cancer cells to normal cells.

5. Lastly, creating your own Second Fermentation flavours is fun and very simple to do. After the initial ferment and the SCOBY is removed the world is your oyster in regards to flavour. Herbal teas can be added as well as fruits, herbs and vegetables and these can all add flavour and nutrient density to your Kombucha.

Considerations When Making Kombucha

The potential healing side effects you may experience when consuming Kombucha have already been mentioned along with the fact that alcohol, although low, is present. The fermentation of the tea does not alter the caffeine content. If you are sensitive to caffeine, I recommend that you dilute the Kombucha when doing a Second fermentation: ¼ Kombucha to ¾ non caffeine drink (herbal tea, water or fruit juice). You can also dilute the Kombucha by drinking it with soda water, filtered water, water Kefir, herbal tea or juice like a cordial, to reduce the caffeine content.

Brewing Kombucha can have a small potential for explosion. To minimize the risk I make the following recommendations:

1. Always keep your Kombucha in a safe area so, if it does explode, it will not endanger anyone or anything.

2. Ferment in an open vessel with plenty of space between the surface of the liquid and the rim of the jar. This reduces the carbon dioxide byproduct from accumulating. I use a wide mouth, 2 litre jar to ferment 1 litre of Kombucha.

3. During the Second Fermentation, always use pressure tested or appropriate bottles if you are going to use a closed vessel ferment. I use and recyle flip top bottles sold for beer fermentation or I brew with open vessels.

4. To get a fizzy drink you can dilute with soda water.

Kombucha tea is very acidic and there have been some concerns about eroding tooth enamel. Personally I believe that the bacterial component of the drink will help to protect the teeth, however if you are worried dilute the Kombucha, drink it through a straw and moderate how much you drink every day.

My young children will drink Kombucha in small amounts, but some parents may be concerned about the acidity and alcohol content of Kombucha. As with everything, monitor how you or your children react when consuming Kombucha and moderate accordingly. Again, by diluting your Kombucha with soda water, filtered water, cooled herbal tea or juice, you may lessen the amount consumed in a day and thus reduce the potential alcohol levels. Allowing kids to experience sour flavours is an excellent way to culture their palate.

Teas to use

The best teas to use when making Kombucha are ones that originate from the tea plant. Black tea, green tea and white tea are all suitable. These teas contain amazing antioxidant properties and really work well with the Kombucha SCOBY. They are also the teas traditionally used when fermenting in this way.

I have also experimented with caffeine free, nutrient dense teas like roobios and tulsi and there may be other options too. I have moderated the brewing time when using roobios and tulsi since these teas require a longer brewing time to form a decent membrane and SCOBY. They also need a higher amount of starter tea (I use 150mls) and may need the addition of more sugar mid brew.

It is important that you constantly monitor SCOBY formation and taste while brewing. I recommend either alternating the teas you use or using the SCOBY's from the tea leaf tea to ferment the other teas for a stronger SCOBY formation.

How to make it

When making Kombucha, each SCOBY and each fermentation will be different, just as it is when making Kefir. Some SCOBY's may be more robust than others and be able to brew herbal teas and adapt to other sugars while some may be more temperamental. Some brewers have even used fruit juice as a sweetener. What is necessary is: tea, sugar and an acidic environment. The amount of sugar is dependent on your taste and the time you leave the Kombucha to ferment. It is possible to brew a strong tea as a concentrate and then water it down (and this will also cool it down). The tea can be sweetened while still hot (when it is easier to get the sugar to dissolve). I use coconut sugar for the First Fermentation then coconut sugar, coconut nectar or maple syrup for the Second Fermentation.

What you will need:

Wide Glass Jar (I use 1.6 litre Jar)
Cooled strong tea (green, black or white)
Cool water
Sugar
Acid (either brewed Kombucha saved from the last batch or 2 tbs of any vinegar)
Plastic tongs (to transport the mother - you can also use fingers)
Piece of cotton or muslin (plus a rubber band to secure)
Plastic funnel and glass bottle for bottling second fermentation
SCOBY Hotel (glass jar in which to keep the mother with some reserved tea)

Ratio

½-1 cup sugar to 1 litre tea
5-10% of amount (so 50-100mls for 1 litre) brewed Kombucha
or 2 tbsp vinegar (I use apple cider vinegar)

Directions

Brew 1 litre of your choice of tea and allow to cool. The tea needs to be at body temperature (no hotter). Add the sugar to the tea while still hot to allow it to dissolve. Taste it - it should taste like overly sweet tea.

Add your 50-100mls of brewed Kombucha tea or 2 tbs of vinegar (any kind) if you have no reserved tea Kombucha from a previous batch.

Then add the 'mother' SCOBY

Always cover the vessel with a light, porous cloth that allows air circulation, but protects from bugs and dust.

Leave vessel in a warm spot, away from direct sunlight.

The length of time for fermentation will depend on the outside temperature and how strong tasting you want your drink to be. Taste it every few days to see if you like it, but on average it should take between 7-14 days (or even up to 8 weeks, depending on the outside temperature).

When it is to your taste, take the mother out and place in a bowl to separate the layers or the 'babies".

Reserve some (50-100mls) of the tea to store in the fridge for the next batch. The cool temperature of the fridge will pause fermentation. Consume the Kombucha neat or dilute it with soda water (as you would with a cordial) or add flavourings of your choice.

Troubleshooting:

Not Fermenting: SCOBY is not viable: solution may have been too hot when you added it or the location where it was stored was too cool. The water quality (if chlorine is present) may be inhibiting it. Also ensure that it is kept still to form a membrane on the surface.

Too Sour: Left too long. Try a shorter fermentation. Can be diluted with carbonated water and more sugar can be added if desired. Fresh Juice is another way of sweetening the Kombucha.

Flavour too weak: Use a more concentrated tea at the beginning. Add more tea bags/leaves to the pot.

Surface mold: Increase starting acidity, i.e. apple cider vinegar or starter tea. Also unsure you use a lid that can breathe (like cloth) otherwise condensation may fall back into the jar an can cause surface mold.

Mother Sinks: Be patient it may rise or an edge will rise causing a new 'mother' to generate on the surface. I normally wait 7 days and taste. If there is no membrane formed or bubbles on the surface I still wait another 4-5 days and reassess. Depending on your room temperature and humidity levels the fermentation can sometimes be slow. Consider placing on top of the fridge or using a heat mat in winter (like that used in a terrarium) if your house is cold.

SECOND FERMENTATION

This secondary fermentation is for flavour and fun! Use fruit or vegetable juice, a sweetened herbal infusion or plain filtered water. Mix in some more sugar (now you can use whatever you want, for example, maple syrup, coconut nectar, raw honey) for carbonation. You can do this second fermentation in an aerobic conditions (as with the first one) or in a sealed air-locked vessel (or in recycled beer flip top bottles!).

In an open aerobic environment, because of the added sugar, you are likely to develop another 'mother' on the surface. In a sealed environment you are likely to get more alcohol (0.5 % which is still considered non-alcoholic) and lactic acid (causing the fizz). Beware of excessive carbonation. Bottles may explode.

Avoid mold by keeping the tea acidic. If you see mold, throw away both the tea and the SCOBY.

I always use an open top vessel to do my second fermentation as the potential for explosion is high. Also, since I use soda water to dilute my Kombucha, I don't need the fizz.

Chapter 4
Kombucha Recipes

Drinks

Chai Roobios and Orange Black Tea Kombucha

INGREDIENTS

2 cups chai roobios tea (add hot water to 2 tea bags or 2 tbsp of loose tea and allow to cool)
2 cups of black tea Kombucha
2 tbsp sugar
½ orange with peel cut into slices

DIRECTIONS

Combine ingredients in an open canister. Cover and leave in a warm, still environment where it will not be disturbed for 7-14 days. Ferment to taste. Remove the new SCOBY if formed and strain the fruit. Dilute with sparkling water and sweeten as necessary.

....

(Also makes a mean cocktail with the addition of a little dark rum and coconut nectar)

Culture Your Life
Kefir and Kombucha For Every Day Nourishment

Ginger Beer Kombucha

INGREDIENTS

2 cups Kombucha (white, green, roobios or black tea)
2 cups filtered water
1 knuckle size piece of ginger (sliced but with the skin on)
1 tbsp ginger coconut sugar (coconut sigar mixed with ginger extract or ground ginger)
Or 1 tbsp coconut sugar and ½ tsp of ground ginger

DIRECTIONS

Combine ingredients in an old resealable beer bottle. Seal and leave in a warm, still environment where it will not be disturbed for 7-14 days. Open from time to time to ensure pressure doesn't build up. Ferment to taste. Remove the new SCOBY if formed and strain the ginger. Dilute with sparkling water and sweeten as necessary.

(Also makes a mean cocktail with the addition of a little dark rum and coconut nectar)

Mango Kombucha

INGREDIENTS

2 cups Kombucha (white, green, roobios or black tea)
2 cups filtered water
2 tbs coconut sugar
½ mango cubed

DIRECTIONS

Combine ingredients in an open canister. Cover and leave in a warm, still environment where it will not be disturbed for 7-14 days. Ferment to taste. Remove the new SCOBY if formed and strain the fruit. Dilute with sparkling water and sweeten as necessary.

Ice Lemon Kombucha Tea

INGREDIENTS

1/2 cup black, roobios or white tea Kombucha
½ cup sparkling water
1 tbs Whole Lemon-ade or similar
Handful of ice

DIRECTIONS

Place all the ingredients in the glass and adjust the amount of lemonade to taste. Sweeten if necessary. Can also be blended with ice to make a slushy.

(Also makes a mean cocktail. To make my Kombucha Long Island Ice Tea, replace Coca Cola with Kombucha, a tbsp of whole lemonade and soda water. Add ¼ shot gin, tequila, vodka and rum).

Scoby Forming on Mixed Berry Second Ferment

Mixed Berry Kombucha with its new SCOBY

Mixed Berry White Tea Kombucha

INGREDIENTS

2 cups white tea Kombucha
2 cups filtered water
2 tbs cococnut sugar
1 handful of frozen or fresh mixed berries

DIRECTIONS

Combine ingredients in an open canister. Cover and leave in a warm, still environment where it will not be disturbed for 7-14 days. Ferment to taste. Remove the new SCOBY if formed and strain the fruit. Dilute with sparkling water and sweeten as necessary.

Apple and Fig White Tea Kombucha

INGREDIENTS

2 cups white tea Kombucha
2 cups water
3 tbsp coconut sugar
½ tsp cinnamon (optional)
Half a peeled and cored fresh apple or 2 tbsp Apple Sauce and 2 figs cubed
Or 4 slices of dehydrated apple and a handful of dried figs

DIRECTIONS

Combine ingredients in an open canister. Cover the mixture and leave in a warm, still environment where it will not be disturbed for 7-14 days. Ferment to taste. Remove the new SCOBY if formed and strain the fruit. Dilute with sparkling water and sweeten as necessary.

....

(Also makes a mean warming cocktail with the addition of a little whisky)

Jasmine and Apple Green Tea Kombucha

INGREDIENTS

2 cups green tea Kombucha
2 cups jasmine tea (made with 2 teabags or loose tea and hot water and left to cool)
3 tbsp coconut sugar
Half a peeled and cored fresh apple, cubed, 2 tbsp Apple Sauce Or 4 slices of dehydrated Apple.

DIRECTIONS

Combine ingredients in an open canister. Cover and leave in a warm, still environment where it will not be disturbed for 7-14 days. Ferment to taste. Remove the new SCOBY if formed and strain the fruit. Dilute with sparkling water and sweeten as necessary.

Scoby

SCOBY Shake

INGREDIENTS

1 Kombucha SCOBY
1 cup favourite juice ingredients
(I use apple, carrot, ginger and kale leaves)
2 cups water Kefir or flavoured Kefir
(May also use juice or filtered water)

DIRECTIONS

Add all ingredients to a high speed blender. The SCOBY tastes just like your neat Kombucha (slightly fizzy and sour). Sweeten if necessary.

Cinnamon SCOBY Crackers

(SCOBY Snacks)

INGREDIENTS

Kombucha SCOBY (sliced with a ceramic knife into squares- you may want to pull them apart so that they are about 0.5cm thick)
1/2 tsp cinnamon (ground)
1 tbsp coconut sugar

DIRECTIONS

Mix the cinnamon and sugar together (taste).

Pick up a square of SCOBY and dust both sides with the sugar and cinnamon

Place on your dehydrator sheet or a greased baking sheet.

Dehydrate at 100 degrees F (to keep bacterial properties of the SCOBY in order to make a probiotic snack) for between 6-12 hours (you may want to turn them mid way).

You can also use the coolest setting on your oven or just the fan- keep the oven door open.

Store in an airtight container and they will last for ages - although if you are like my kids they will be gone in seconds!

These are my daughter's favourite snack.

....

Here are some suggestions for other flavours;

Marinade in coconut aminos (or soy sauce), garlic, ginger and coconut sugar for a teriyaki SCOBY snack

Marinade in fresh apple and carrot juice before powdering with coconut sugar

Stir in Tabasco or chili flakes and coconut sugar for a hot sweet and sour hit!

Kombucha Salad Dressing

To make any basic dressing you need vinegar, oil, something sour like lemon juice and something sweet like raw honey or coconut sugar.

This is my base recipe I call it Kombucharette instead of a vinegarette;

INGREDIENTS

1 tbs Kombucha
Juice of half a lemon
2 tbsp avocado oil or walnut oil
Salt and pepper to season
1 tsp coconut sugar

HONEY MUSTARD DRESSING

3-4 tbsp base recipe (the amount above)
1 tsp Dijon Mustard/whole grain mustard
1 tsp raw honey (adjust to taste)

ASIAN DRESSING;

3-4 tbsp of the base recipe (use sesame/garlic oil as optional)
Pinch of ground ginger
1 tsp coconut aminos or soy sauce
1 tsp sesame seeds
Pinch chilli flakes

DIRECTIONS

Mix all the ingredients together in a small mason jar, put on the lid and shake to emulsify each time you use it.

House

Why is Kombucha such a good cleaning product?

I use vinegar to clean my children's re-useable nappies and our clothes most of the time. So one day, when we ran out of vinegar, I tried Kombucha instead. Everything (especially the nappies) came out so clean that I always use it now. I also noticed how good the Kombucha was at cleaning our white counter tops and sink. I then played with some ideas for the tub and toilet. The following recipes are the ones we use everyday at home.

This makes sense. Kombucha has similar acids to those in apple cider vinegar and is naturally antiseptic and antimicrobial, making it a safe and effective cleaner. It can be used as a fruit and vegetable wash (it cuts through the fat soluble chemicals in pesticides); as a washing detergent (it works well on dirt, sweat and fat stains on clothes) and it deodorises cloth nappies, much like other vinegars. This makes Kombucha a cheap, environmentally friendly and easy product to use around the house.

Fruit Wash

INGREDIENTS

½ bottle Kombucha
½ bottle filtered water
(Depending on size of bottle)

DIRECTIONS

Add Kombucha and water to a spray bottle. Fill bowl or sink with filtered water. Spray the mixture liberally on the water. Allow fruits and vegetables to soak for a few minutes and then drain. If washing soft fruits or leafy greens, spray directly on the fruit and then gently rinse and dry by leaving on a towel.

All Purpose Cleaner

INGREDIENTS

½ Kombucha
½ water
juice of 1/2 a lemon
10 drops lavender

DIRECTIONS

Add to a spray bottle or use an old general purpose cleaning spray bottle that has been washed well. Use on all surfaces. Great on glass and tiles. (Do a spot test first if worried, especially on varnished wood.)

Washing detergent

INGREDIENTS

2 tbsp Kombucha (any)
10 drops of lavender in the rinse compartment (optional)

DIRECTIONS

Add to the detergent dispenser of your washing machine.

Use the washing machine at 30 or 40 degrees to maintain bacterial action.

Spot Remover

INGREDIENTS

½ tsp Kombucha (any)
1 tsp baking powder

DIRECTIONS

Rub baking powder onto the spot and add drops of Kombucha. Rub well into the stain and leave to dry. Wash as normal. This can also then be soaked in water for a hour or so.

Bath, Sink & Toilet Cleaner

INGREDIENTS

1/2 tsp Kombucha
1 tbsp baking soda
pinch of salt
10 drops of lavender (or tea tree oil)

DIRECTIONS

Add baking powder to an old cleaning bottle that has been washed well. Add the rest of the ingredients slowly since baking powder fizzes and bubbles. Add the mixture to the toilet or bath and use a brush to scrub if necessary. Leave to dry. When dry, rinse off.

Support Recipes

Raw Almond Milk

INGREDIENTS

1 cup almonds
3 cups filtered water
1-3 medjool dates (optional sweetener)
Pinch of salt (I have been using Pink Himalayan rock salt but I also like sea salt)
Vanilla and almond essence (optional)

DIRECTION

You have to soak the almonds first overnight or for at least 8 hours. I use raw almonds to get the most nutrition and I soak them in filtered water.

When the almonds are ready, put all the ingredients in a blender with the water.

I blend, pulse, then blend again to make sure I get as much out of the almonds as possible. I then strain through a nut/soup bag. I have also used a sieve as I don't mind fine bits of almond in my milk. To get a smoother consistency you can use the nut bag or a muslin cloth.

I then dry the almonds in the dehydrator or the lowest setting in the oven (or just use the fan in your oven if you can) for up to 12 hours until completely dry. This raw almond milk can be used as is or can be used to make Almond Milk Kefir. Just add the milk or water grains and leave, covered with muslin, for 8-24 hours. Ferment to taste!

....

You can substitute other nuts/seeds for the almonds. Try some different combinations such as the following:

Hazelnut and Almond
Cashew and Hazelnut
Sesame seed (no need to strain this milk)
Pumpkin seed and Sunflower seed
Hemp Seed (no need to strain this milk)
Cashew and Almond
Brazil nut

Raw Oat Milk

An oat groat is the whole grain of the oat, the starting point from which it undergoes processes to become rolled oats. Since it has had less processes than a rolled oat it retains a higher nutritional value. You have to soak the groats first overnight or for at least 8 hours. I use raw groats to get the most nutrition and I soak them in filtered water.

When the Groats are ready I strain them, discarding the water, and then put them in a blender. These, along with the following ingredients and the following ratio:

1 cup oat groats: 3 cups of filtered water.

INGREDIENTS

1 cup of soaked oat groats/rolled oats
3 cups filtered water
a pinch of salt
(I have been using pink Himalayan rock salt but I also like sea salt)
2 drops vanilla essence
1-2 medjool dates (optional)

DIRECTION

I blend, pulse and then blend again to make sure I get as much out of the oat groats as possible. I then strain through a nut/soup bag to get a smoother consistency but this is optional. Just add the milk or water grains and leave, covered with muslin, for 8-24 hours. Ferment to taste!

Raw Coconut Milk

I use young Thai coconuts because I love their taste. Other, older meat may need straining and there are also several methods of making coconut milk from dried coconut. In the tropics we can find these in abundance in the supermarkets and I love using the water and the meat to get a nutritious milk.

INGREDIENTS

1 1/2 cups of coconut water (roughly the contents of 1 coconut)

1 1/2 cups of filtered water

1 cup of coconut meat (normally 2-3 coconuts' worth)

DIRECTION

Add all your ingredients to a blender and blend until thick and creamy. No need to strain! This will keep in the fridge for at least a week or you can also make Coconut milk Kefir from this. Just add the milk or water grains and leave, covered with muslin, for 8-24 hours. Ferment to taste!

....

An even easier way to make coconut milk is to open a coconut and blend the water and meat together. (add a little filtered water if necessary)

Chia Porridge

INGREDIENTS

3 tbsp chia seeds
1 cup Almond, Oat or Coconut milk or any Kefir
1/2-1 tsp cinnamon
1/2 tsp vanilla essence
diced strawberries, raspberries, figs & blueberries

Coconut Yoghurt
raw almonds, cashews, sesame & sunflower seeds for toppings (preferably soaked over night)

DIRECTIONS

Place milk in a bowl and sprinkle in the chia seeds. Stir immediately for a minute or so to avoid clumping. Add spices as you stir, together with the vanilla. Allow to stand for 10-20 mins to thicken, or leave covered in the fridge overnight. Add yoghurt, berries, nuts and seeds to taste.

Raw Jam

INGREDIENTS

1 ½ cups of fruit
(mango, cherries, peaches, blueberries, strawberries)
2 tbs chia seeds
1 tbs of water.

Depending on what consistency you like for your jam (rough or smooth) you can either mash the fruit flesh or blitz it in the blender with the water. Add to a jar. Mix in the chia seeds and place in the fridge to 'set'. I'm not kidding it's as easy as that. I love it. You can use most fruit. Experiment!

Chocolate Avocado Pudding

INGREDIENTS

4 very ripe avocados
3-6 medjool dates (to taste)
2 tbs raw cacao
1 tsp water
Vanilla essence
Pinch of salt

DIRECTIONS

Place all the ingredients in a food blender. Blitz until smooth. If you need to, sweeten to taste by adding coconut sugar, maple syrup or more dates. Serve. Freeze in silicon cupcake cases or an ice cube tray for use in Rocky Road Kefir Ice Cream or in Chocolate Avocado Pudding Kefir Shake.

Culture Your Life
Kefir and Kombucha For Every Day Nourishment

Homemade Chocolate

INGREDIENTS

1 cup of coconut oil (or half coconut oil, half cocoa butter)
1 cup raw cacao powder (or half powder and half raw cacao nibs for a chocolate chip consistancy)
1 tbs coconut sugar sweeten to taste with coconut nectar/sugar or maple syrup
You can also use 3 pitted medjool dates
vanilla essence

DIRECTIONS

Blend in a food processor or stir in a measuring jug. Either lay out onto greaseproof paper in a shallow baking tin or use small chocolate molds or silicon cupcake cases. Place in the freezer and freeze until hard (between 30 mins to an hour). Break into pieces and store in a glass container in the fridge.

....

You can add anything to this basic mix to flavour your chocolate. Here are some suggested combinations:

1 tbs nut butter
Dried fruit and nuts
Dried coconut
Mint essence
Dried Orange peel
Bee pollen
Ground ginger
Chilli flakes

Whole Lemon-ade

INGREDIENTS

1 whole lemon (organic and un-waxed)

3 cups of water

4 tsp coconut sugar (optional- to taste)

DIRECTIONS

I make this in my high speed blender as it is necessary to process the peel, pith, skin and pips. I use 4 tsp of coconut sugar as I like my lemons tart. Whizz it all up and then use it like a cordial. I add fizzy water and ice to mine and I also use it in Iced Lemon Kombucha Tea. Store any unused quantity in the fridge.

Apple Sauce

INGREDIENTS

500g apples
1tbp cinnamon
1/2 tsp rock salt
1/4 cup of filtered water

DIRECTION

Core and peel the apples and cut them into small pieces, place in a saucepan. Keep the peel to make your own apple cider vinegar. Add the cinnamon and season with a pinch of the salt. Add 2 tbs of water at a time when necessary.

Cook on a low heat until soft and starting to go mushy. Lightly mash (or puree, however you like the texture. I like it with a little bite still). Season to taste.

....

This can be made in advance and stored in a jar. Optional variations include using a little lemon juice and/or butter at the end.

You can also add all the ingredients to a slow cooker and cook on low for 2-4 hours. This way you can keep the peel on the apples.

Resources

References

Campbell-McBride, Dr Natasha (2010) *Gut and Psychology Syndrome* Medinform

Rosa Krajmalnik-Brown, P. Z.-E.-W. (2012, Feb 24th). *Effects of Gut Microbes on Nutrient Absorption and Energy Regulation. Nutr Clin Pract.*

Kelly, D, T. King, R. Aminov (2007). *Importance of microbial colonization of the gut in early life to the development of immunity.* Mutat Res. 2007 Sep 1;622(1-2):58-69. Epub 2007 Apr 6.

James, Walene *PASTEURIAN GERM THEORY vs BECHAMP CELLULAR THEORY* web article (June 2014) http://www.whale.to/v/germ.htm

Rosa Krajmalnik-Brown, P. Z.-E.-W. (2012, Feb 24th). *Effects of Gut Microbes on Nutrient Absorption and Energy Regulation. Nutr Clin Pract.*

http://www.organic.org/home/faq

Katz, Sandor E (2012) *The Art of Fermentation* Chelsea Green

http://www.icap.org/table/alcoholbeveragelabeling

Kefir – a complex probiotic 2006 *Food Science and Technology Bulletin: Fu, Volume 2* http://www.kefir.it/kefir_probiotic.pdf

Works Cited

PASTEURIAN GERM THEORY vs BECHAMP CELLULAR THEORY

*Gut and Psychology Syndrome: Natural Treatment for Autism, Dyspraxia, A.D.D., Dyslexia, A.D.H.D., Depression, Schizophrenia*2010Medinform Publishing

Kefir – a complex probiotic2006*Food Science and Technology Bulletin: Fu, Volume 2* 1 microbiological and chemical properties of kefir manufactured by entrapped microorganisms isolated from kefir grains 2009 *American Dairy Science Association*

Rawlings, D. (2013). *Fermented Foods For Health.* Fair Winds Press.

Rosa Krajmalnik-Brown, P. Z.-E.-W. (2012, Feb 24th). Effects of Gut Microbes on Nutrient Absorption and Energy Regulation. *Nutr Clin Pract. Author manuscript* .

The gut microbiota as an environmental factor that regulates fat storage 2004 *Proc Natl Acad Sci U.S.A 101 (44)* 15718-15723

http://www.ewg.org/foodnews/summary.php

http://www.whale.to/v/germ.htm

https://www.ncbi.nlm.nih.gov/pubmed/17612575

http://www.ncbi.nlm.nih.gov/pmc/articles/PMC3601187/

http://www.organic.org/home/faq

http://www.smallfootprintfamily.com/hybrid-seeds-vs-gmos

http://www.foodrenegade.com/just-say-no-to-uht-milk/

http://www.kefir.it/kefir_probiotic.pdf

http://www2.hcmuaf.edu.vn/data/lhquang/file/Tea1/Tea,%20Kombucha,%20and%20health.pdf

http://www.kombuchakamp.com/2011/09/kombucha-side-effects-herxheimer-reaction-healing-crisis.html

Cummings , J.H , G.T. Macfarlane *Role of intestinal bacteria in nutrient* metabolism

Medical Research Council Dunn Clinical Nutrition Centre, Hills Road, Cambridge CB2 2DH, UK

Nutr Clin Pract. 2012 Apr;27(2):201-14. doi: 10.1177/0884533611436116. Epub 2012 Feb 24.

Krajmalnik-Brown R, Ilhan ZE, Kang DW, DiBaise JK Effects of gut microbes on nutrient absorption and energy regulation.

Biodesign Institute at Arizona State University, Tempe, Arizona, USA.

http://www.icap.org/table/alcoholbeveragelabeling

Backhed, F. H. Ding, T. Wang et al (2004) *The gut microbiota as an environmental factor that regulates fat storage.* Proc Natl Acad Sci U.S.A 101 (44); 15718-15723

Beuchat, L. R (2012) 13 indiginous fermented foods

http://www.wiley-vch.de/books/biotech/pdf/v09indig.pdf

Books

Blaser, Martin (2014) *Missing Microbes: How Killing Bacteria Creates Modern Plagues* Oneworld

Campbell-McBride, Dr Natasha (2010) *Gut and Psychology Syndrome* Medinform

Ciciarelli, Jill (2013) *Fermented- a four season approach to Paleo probiotic foods*

Fallon, Sally and Mary G. Enig (2001) *Nourishing Traditions; The cookbook that challenges politically correct and the diet dictocrats* New Trends Publishing

Harmon, Wardeh (2007) *The Complete Idiots Guide to Fermenting Foods* Alpha Books

Huffnagle, Gary B with Sarah Wernick *The Probiotics Revolution; The Definitive Guide to Safe, Natural Health Solutions Using PRobiotic and Prebiotic Foods and Supplements* Bantam

Katz, Sandor E (2012) *The Art of Fermentation* Chelsea Green

Katz, Sandor E *Wild Fermentation* Chelsea Green

Kaufmann, Klaus (1997) *Kefir Rediscovered: The Nutritional Benefits of an Ancient Healing Food* Alive Books

Lewin, Alex (2003) *Real Food Fermentation; Preserving Whole Fresh Food with Live Cultures in Your Home Kitchen* Quarry Books

Rawlings, Deidre (2013) *Fermented Foods For Health; Use the Power os Probiotic Foods to Improve Your Digestion, Strengthen Your Immunity and Prevent Illness* Fair Winds Press

Tietz, Harald (1996) *Kefir: For Pleasure and Wellbeing* Harald Tietze Publishing PL

Ziedrich, Linda (2009) *The Joy of Pickling 250 Flavor Packed Recipes for Vegetables and More from Garden or Market.* Harvard Common Press

Websites with Information and Recipes;

Balanced Bites
balancedbites.com
Chris Kresser
chriskresser.com
Dom's How to make Kefir and recipes;
http://users.sa.chariot.net.au/~dna/Makekefir.html#preparingfibres
Fearless Eating
fearlesseating.net
Fermenters Club
fermentersclub.com
Food Swap Network
foodswapnetwork.com
Kombucha Fuel
kombuchafuel.com
Kombucha Kamp
kombuchakamp.com
Lantau Mama
lantaumama.com
Loula Natural
loulanatural.com
The Nourishing Cook
Thenourishingcook.com
Nourished Kitchen
nourishedkitchen.com
Oh Lardy
ohlardy.com
Weston A Price
westonaprice.org
Wild Fermentation
wildfermentation.com

Web Stores to get Cultures

First try to find out at your local health food shops of holistic health centre if there are any local fermenters or classes to give you grains. Grains are often shared and there are several fermenting groups and forums online who can help you to get some heritage grains. If not the following information is useful.

In the U.S.A

Cultures for Health
culturesforhealth.com
Kombucha Kamp
kombuchakamp.com
Organic Cultures
organic-cultures.com
Real Kefir Grains
kefirlady.com
Royal Kombucha
royakombucha.com
Wise Choice Market
wisechoicemarket.com

In the UK

The Kefir Company
thekefircompany.co.uk
Happy Kombucha
happykombucha.co.uk
Buy Kefir
buy-kefir.co.uk
Nourish Kefir
nourishkefir.co.uk
Kefir Shop
kefirshop.co.uk

In Australia

Nourish Me Organics
nourishmeorganics.com
Kefir Magic
kefirmagic.com
Fresh Milk Kefir
freshmilkkefirgrains.com

FURTHER READING

Ackerman, Jennifer 2012 *How bacteria in our bodies protect our health*. Scientific American (May)

Gershon, M (1999) *The second brain; A groundbreaking new understanding of nervous disorders of the stomach and intestines* New York; Harper Perenial

Hiroaki Maeda, Xia Zhu, Kazunobu Omura, Shiho Suzuki, Shinichi Kitamura (2004) *Effects of an exopolysaccharide (kefiran) on lipids, blood pressure, blood glucose, and constipation* BioFactors, Volume 22, Numbers 1-4, pages 197-200

Fabian, J.C , J.L Sandrine et al (2012) Milk fermented by propionibacrerium freudenreichii *induces apoptosis of HGT-1 human gastric cancer cells. Plos ONE 7(3); e31892. Doi;10;1371/journal. pome.0031892*

Sahlin, Peter (1999) Fermentation as a method of food processing *Lund Institute of Technology, Dept, Food Chemisty (May) Thesis (as seens on http://www.eden-foundation.org/project/articles_fermentation_thesis.pdf June2014)*

Lee, Y.K and S. K. Mazmanian (2010) Has the microbiota played a critical role in the evolution of the adaptive immune system? *Science 330:1768-1773*

Kelly, D, T. King, R. Aminov (2007).*Importance of microbial colonization of the gut in early life to the development of immunity.* Mutat Res. 2007 Sep 1;622(1-2):58-69. Epub 2007 Apr 6.

The Germ Theory of Disease Causation as seen on http://tuberose.com/Germ_Theory.html (June 2014)

file:///C:/Users/USER/Downloads/Pogacic_et_al__Microbiota_of_kefir_grains.pdf